those who
trust
the
Lord
SHALL NOT BE
DISAPPOINTED

Those Who Trust the Lord Shall Not Be Disappointed

©2003 by Peggy Joyce Ruth, BETTER LIVING Ministries
www.peggyjoyceruth.org

Printed in the United States of America
ISBN #0-89228-174-X

Cover designed by Andrea Verano of Brownwood, Texas.

Scripture references are taken from the
New American Standard Bible,
Copyright 1960, 1963, 1968, 1971, 1972, 1973, 1975, 1977
by The Lockman Foundation. Used by permission.

2003 1st Printing
2003 2nd Printing
2008 3rd Printing
2009 4th Printing

Dear Reader,

Last year, Lorraine and I (she's directly in front of me in the picture that follows) read the book *Those Who Trust in the Lord Shall not be Disappointed* by Peggy Joyce Ruth. The book was primarily about how the Lord is faithful to His Word; and it related testimony after testimony of how she and her family took the Lord seriously about His ability to meet their needs as they trusted Him in specific ways.

In particular, they were not disappointed in His miraculous provision of a home in a very unique way. The book was a catalyst for our faith. I was being transferred from a sea duty assignment in Florida to shore duty in Washington, DC. We were going to need a house that would permit a seven children, home schooling family to have a bit of elbowroom.

We got the whole family around the kitchen table and set up the whiteboard to capture ideas. I asked each person in the family to list our needs and desires for a home in our next duty station. We also listed ministry areas in which we have been led to serve as a family and to which our home situation would serve us in complementary fashion. We listed over 30 desires and needs for our home. Most on the list were desires.

From the list I wrote up a Mayflower Compact type covenant, specifically covenanting with the Lord about our move to Washington, DC, and how our family would be used of the Lord in His purposes. We prayed frequently as a family, lifting this compact up to the Lord, reminding Him that we trusted Him to meet our needs and thanking Him for what He would do.

We packed up and drove from Florida at the end of July without any worldly reason to have hope in finding the house we needed. We arrived at the Anacostia Navy housing office in Washington, DC on August 2nd and were told what we had heard before. They had no available large quarters for us and asked if we would like to see the rental market listing. I asked if there might be something unusual available—could they think "out-of-the-box" for other options. Perhaps on a military base further out from Washington, D.C.

The lady called several different distant bases with no success. Then she called the Navy base at Indian Head in Maryland, about 45 minutes south of downtown Washington, D.C. Her eyes brightened as she spoke on the phone. Sure enough, they had a big house that was available now—it was an old house and had eight bedrooms. I was excited that this might be our provision from the Lord.

We drove immediately to Indian Head to investigate. As we drove up to the house, we noticed instantly that one of our desires was answered. It had a wrap around front porch! We also noted that another desire, almost too embarrassing to ask for, was also granted: the house had a beautiful panoramic view of the Potomac River! **The next 15 minutes revealed the Lord had provided every single one of the 30+ specific requests we had laid before Him.** With tears, we stopped and worshiped and thanked the Lord for His goodness to us. The cheery house we now live in is 112 years old and has all the room we need. Lorraine is pleased to be able to fully unpack all our belongings for the first time in almost four years. As a bonus, it is even on a golf course with an adjacent tennis court. **Is anything too difficult for GOD?**

—Thomas H. "Hank" Bond, Jr.
Captain; U.S. Navy

Contents

Preface

My phone started ringing early one morning before I even had a chance to get dressed. As soon as I picked it up, Sandy Black from Arkansas came on the line and asked me to speak at the Christian Women's Club in El Dorado. I had heard of the great success they were having in unifying the Christian women of their city, and it was impressive. Practically every denomination was actively involved, and they had already outgrown three previous locations.

I was honored to be asked to come, but also quite humbled at the prospect. With only one hour, what could I say to such a diverse group of people, from so many different backgrounds, that would affect their lives? I felt that more than likely this would be my only opportunity to ever address this group of ladies, and more than anything I wanted it to count for something worthwhile. I had been in too many meetings when, after two days, no one could even remember the original topic much less the content. I wanted God to send me with a message that would still be burning in their hearts two years later.

I had already begun a search through my Bible to find some memorable theme when suddenly the Lord impressed me with the question, "What is the most valuable thing you have ever learned?" At that moment I knew exactly which message I would take to El Dorado.

Two things stood out immediately for having had the greatest life-changing effect on my Christian growth. One was God's covenant from the ninety-first Psalm. I have since written a book on that revelation, entitled *Psalm 91 God's Umbrella of Protection.* And equally as influential on my life has been the revelation God had given me on *Those who Trust the Lord will not be Disappointed.*

God was indeed faithful in His answer to my prayer. That message was not forgotten two days after it was delivered. In fact, it was not forgotten two years after it was delivered! I was invited back to El Dorado for the next two years, and the women thronged me with report after report of how their lives had been changed by that message. In fact, several of the ladies specifically said, "We have been trusting God and we truly have not been disappointed!" And the person who introduced me that day said, "We are happy to have the Trust-in-the-Lord-and-not-be-disappointed lady back!"

My prayer is that this Truth, with a capital T, will revolutionize your life and be as meaningful to you. However, what I hope to say in these pages is not exactly a traditional Bible teaching. It is one continuous witness of how this simple truth became the foundation of my own personal faith and that of my family, and it is power packed with exciting testimonies of miracle after miracle that demonstrate God's steadfast love and constant care.

Many years have now passed since the day I first began to trust Him, without reservation, exactly as He tells us to do. And not a single day has passed in which I have not had cause to thank Him for the way He keeps His promises and honors His commitments.

—Peggy Joyce Ruth

Foreword

First Peter 2:6 tells us that those who trust in the Lord shall not be disappointed. What an incredible statement! But does it apply in daily life? Will it work for every member of the family? Can it be applied seven days a week throughout the year? In other words, is it an absolute that is tried, proven, and workable on every occasion, or is it just for Dad, Mom, or Grandmother?

More important, who made this wonderful promise and is His Word dependable? Or should we think of it simply as a proposition that may come true on rare occasions, producing a miracle because God might favor us by doing something special just this once? Is it merely an exception that He owes to us as a reward for being obedient children? Or is it, in fact, a covenant that is ours to keep, to claim, and to see fulfilled on a daily basis? Peggy Joyce Ruth's previous book, *Psalm 91 God's Umbrella of Protection,* was tremendously faith building. When we offered it in *Christ for the Nations Magazine* (May, 2002), we received more orders than we had for any other premium in our fifty-five-year history.

Now Peggy Ruth has written this equally important book entitled *Those Who Trust in the Lord Shall Not Be Disappointed,* based on I Peter 2:6–8. In it she shows that this is not a random remark but is, instead, a true covenant that God offers anyone who honestly and sincerely responds. And God always keeps His half of any covenant He enters into.

Peggy chronicles the reality of this truth through the amazing events of her own life and the lives of her husband, son, and daughter, as they personally experienced the reality of this covenant. In every aspect of their lives—in building their home, in seeking God's will for their business and ministry, in rearing their children, and in recreation and rest—they have based their lives on this principle and have been greatly blessed.

This book is both inspiring and practical, to say the least. To practice its precepts will lighten your life. You'll love it!

—Freda Lindsay
Co-Founder of Christ for the Nations
August, 2003

Introduction

Introductions to books are supposed to be written by their authors, and editors are supposed to remain anonymous. On the other hand, this book could turn a lot of our thinking upside down so maybe it's okay to start out a little differently, too.

I printed the original text for this book from an electronic file and read it during a long layover in the Portland airport. It took about ten minutes for me to begin dabbing at my eyes, and only a little bit longer for the people around me to decide that I was either crazy or beside myself with grief. Neither of those assumptions was true, of course, but sometimes our emotions are more confusing to others than they are to ourselves. I knew exactly what I was feeling—and why.

This book was speaking directly to me and my needs, as few others have done. It came into my possession at a time when I desperately needed to hear what it says. However, in that respect I don't think I'm especially unusual. I believe that the message of this book will resonate profoundly within the spirit of every single reader. So, let me see if I can identify what I think makes it so special, by explaining what I had reacted to over and over by the time I finished the last page.

First of all, Peggy Joyce Ruth has chosen to illustrate her message most profusely, with fascinating stories about what happened to real people, in a real family, when they made real, on-purpose decisions to trust God exactly as he invites all of us to do. That it was her own family and her own life makes each of these stories all the more authentic and effective. It's hard to get any closer to the truth than what comes to you through your own eyes and ears. Truly, Peggy Joyce knows what she's talking about from personal experience, not theoretical postulating.

Second, Peggy Joyce clearly identifies the simple, twofold nature of the covenant with Himself that God wants for all of us. Ever since He first began laying out His eternal plan back in the early pages of Genesis, and extending and expanding on it throughout all the rest of His Word, we encounter the same dynamic over and over again: "If you will do as I request, then I will do as I promise and you won't be able to contain the blessings."

Entering into covenant with God is not like driving down a one-way street. On the contrary, it's very much a two-way Avenue of Fulfillment. The only difference is that traffic from the other direction doesn't knock you down and run you over. It meets you on your side of the middle, lifts you up, and carries you to places you could never go by yourself.

Third—and perhaps most important of all—Peggy Joyce makes it equally clear that Trust is not an emotion. You don't have to feel like it—you simply have to decide to do it and proclaim your decision accordingly, at which point God steps immediately into the picture. In this respect, the dynamic involved in trusting God is remarkably similar to the dynamic involved in forgiving others, both of which we are commanded to do in the Scriptures. And in each case we are given far-reaching, life-changing promises detailing what He will do in return, which is always far more than we could ever ask if we were cataloging our most fervent desires!

This is the fundamental God/man dynamic at its most personal, most powerful, and yet most pragmatic level. And yes—that last word might seem a little out of place in a discussion of God's character, but in addition to all the other wonderful things that "God is" He is a God of honor who never breaks a promise and never gives less than a thousand times more than He gets. Likewise, He never changes His mind, or His nature, or the eternal game plan whose rules are so simple yet just as immutable as He is.

He is not a will-o'-the-wisp God in any sense whatsoever. Neither is He fickle, fraudulent, or fictional. He is the only God in the Universe who could bless Peggy Joyce Ruth with the truths and the memories that she shares in this book, and the only one who could make me cry at the sheer joy of recognizing that God has spoken to her so she could speak to me.

And to you.

—Michael Christopher
April, 2008

Left to Right: Peggy Joyce,
David Schum, Angie Schum,
Jack Ruth, Sloan Ruth, Bill Ruth

One Significant Morning

My head shot straight up off the pillow. Was it a noise or had it just been a dream? Scanning my memory and discovering no recent reveries of any significance, I peeked through the blinds to find only the dog stretched out sleepily in the early morning sun. Obviously, whatever had startled me had been my own imagination, yet I sensed that something was different about this particular morning.

A quick glance at the bedside alarm clock let me know that there was no time to lie there and ponder my feelings. Laying aside all reasoning I let my feet hit the floor, not knowing that a new chapter in my life was about to begin. Little did I realize that this day would open a whole new avenue of truth that would help shape my future in a way that very few other things had ever done.

I was soon so busy getting breakfast for my husband, Jack, and our two children, Angelia and Bill, that I scarcely noticed the thought that floated quietly through my mind the first time—*"Those who trust the Lord will not be disappointed."*

Very soon, after everyone had gone out the door, each one headed toward his respective destination, the thought came through a little stronger—*"Those who trust the Lord will not be disappointed!"* Still distracted by my busy schedule I was still not paying much attention to that recurring thought, until it became an almost audible voice. To my knowledge I had never remembered reading that scripture in the Bible. Or was it a scripture? Where was a thought like that coming from?

The Search Begins

All day I found myself almost subconsciously quoting that same phrase over and over again—"Those who trust the Lord will not be disappointed." But by afternoon it was no longer subconscious. I realized something very unusual was happening. Finally, my lightning-fast mind recognized that God was giving me something important that He wanted me to hear!

By this time my curiosity had come into play, and I began to search through my Bible until I found the passage from 1 Peter that I've quoted below, from the *New American Standard Bible*. At that point I was completely hooked, and I soon found myself in the middle of a full-fledged Bible search. The *King James Version* of 1 Peter 2:6 said *"he that believeth on him shall not be confounded,"* but when I looked up that verse in *Strong's New*

Testament Greek Concordance I found that the word translated there as *confounded* also meant "ashamed" or "disappointed." The Lord was obviously dealing with me in the area of disappointment.

I would not have considered myself a person prone to disappointment. However, over the next few days the Lord began to show me that most Christians never go on to get total victory in any area, because at some point they get disappointed. And even though they may never consciously realize it, deep down most disappointments are disappointments in God, whereby a person subconsciously thinks that God didn't come through for them. Or, that He let them down in some area.

In my search through the Bible to find out what God had to say about disappointment, the first scripture to which I was led did not seem to fit the subject.

> *"And blessed is he who keeps from*
> *stumbling over Me."*
> *(Matthew 11:6, NASB, 1973)*

However, though I had always prayed not to stumble I couldn't quite see what stumbling had to do with disappointment. So God led me next to the portion of scripture in which Peter was quoting from the prophet Isaiah:

> 6 *For this is contained in Scripture:*
> *"Behold, I lay in Zion a choice stone, a*
> *precious corner stone,* **and he who believes**
> **in him will not be disappointed."**
>
> 7 *This precious value, then, is for you who*
> *believe; but for those who disbelieve, "The*
> *stone which the builders rejected, this became*
> *the very corner stone,"*
>
> 8 *and, "a stone of stumbling and a rock of*
> *offense"; for they stumble because they are*
> *disobedient to the word, and to this doom*
> *they were also appointed. (I Peter 2:6-8)*

Suddenly I realized why Matthew 11:6 said what it did, and what it had to do with disappointment. First Peter 2:6-8 very plainly says, "He who believes in Him (i.e., 'He who *trusts* in Him') will not be disappointed." And then it goes right on to say that the one who does *not* trust in Him will become disappointed, making the Rock [Jesus, the Word] become a *Stone (or a Rock) of stumbling.*

In other words, any time disappointment is allowed in we get offended with someone or some thing and we begin to stumble. It is *choosing not to be disappointed* that keeps us anchored in trust, and *trust is the state of being that keeps us from stumbling.*

It Starts with Trust

Now . . . let's talk about trust for a moment. Trust in God takes in more than just our eternal salvation. Godly trust starts with the new birth experience when we trust Him as our Savior, but if we do not learn to trust God in every area of life we will eventually, at some point, become subconsciously disappointed in God and when that happens the Rock becomes a Rock of stumbling. In other words, the Word becomes a stumbling block.

The Lord showed me a perfect example of this in John 6:53, when Jesus told His followers that unless they were willing to eat His flesh and drink His blood they would have no life in them. They didn't understand (verse 60) and were unwilling to trust Him; therefore, the Word became a stumbling block to them. Verse 66 tells us that as a result of this teaching many of His disciples withdrew and were not walking with Him any more. A spiritual stumbling always comes as a result of lack of trust in God.

Having long been determined to guard myself from stumbling in my walk with God—perhaps even fearing it to some extent from having watched others fall away—I was ready to hear everything that God had to show me about disappointment. I began to search through the Word and found this truth about disappointment reiterated over and over—*those who trust the Lord shall not be disappointed*—shall not stumble! Twice in the same letter to the Romans Paul quoted from the Old Testament, admonishing the people in Rome that their best protection against stumbling in their faith would be in continuing to keep their trust in God fresh and alive.

> *Just as it is written, behold, I lay in Zion*
> *a stone of stumbling and a rock of offense,*
> *and He who **believes** [i.e., trusts] in Him*
> *will not be disappointed.*
> > *(Romans 9:33, emphasis added)*

> *For the scripture says, "Whoever believes*
> *in Him will not be disappointed."*
> > *(Romans 10:11)*

Even the Psalms taught this same truth!

> *In Thee they trusted and were not disappointed.*
> > *(Psalm 22:5)*

I found this truth paraphrased over and over throughout the Old and New Testament, and in several places it was a direct quote: *Those who trust in the Lord will not be disappointed.* Very few promises are repeated that many times. Obviously the Lord wanted me to get that message fully embedded down in my spirit, but little did I know just how much it was going to change the direction of my life!

I remember arguing, "But Lord, I think I do trust you, but sometimes the Word looks like it's not working, and I get confused, and even disappointed . . .but that doesn't mean I'm not trusting You!" That's when the Lord began to show me that trust and disappointment are exact opposites. And just as fear and faith are opposites and cannot operate at the same time, trust and disappointment cannot both operate at the same time.

Notice the tenses in this scripture! Those who trust (*trusting* is present tense) shall not be disappointed (*shall not be* is future tense). This is a promise with a condition, meaning that if we trust and continue to trust (in the present), every single time we won't be disappointed (in the future).

On the other hand, it does not say that opportunities for disappointment won't present themselves. Temptations to doubt the Lord will come. That's a fact! But when those opportunities come the ball is then in your court. The decision is yours, and it becomes your choice to either (1) fall for the opportunity to be disappointed or (2) to continue to trust God no matter what things look like at the moment, trusting that the time will come when you are truly not disappointed.

That boggled my mind at first, but I have since found it to be an absolute truth. *Those who trust in the Lord shall not be disappointed—literally*. But, trusting is the prerequisite before we see the outcome.

You Don't Have to Feel Like It!

The next big question in my mind was, "How can I know if I am operating in trust?" The Lord showed me that I should turn it around and look at it from the opposite direction. If I found myself wallowing in feelings of disappointment then I would know that I was not operating in Trust. That became my barometer.

The Lord began to show me that we make it much harder than it needs to be. We try to make trust an *emotion*. We struggle and strive to try to muster up *feelings* of trust, yet that is not true trust! Trust, just like faith, starts by simply making an irrevocable decision to believe God's Word, then reclining in His arms and leaving the rest to Him.

Trust is a decision! It is not a feeling! Trust is also a resolution that we activate when we say to God, from our hearts:

> *I don't care what the situation looks like. I don't care what my reasoning ability is dictating to me— I am just not going there! And I also don't care if it looks as though You didn't come through. I don't care what the world says. I don't care what negative reports come down the pike. I don't care what my emotions are dictating; I have made up my mind that from this day forth I am going to steadfastly trust*

what You have said. I will be obedient to do what You tell me to do; I will make Your Word my final authority; and then I will rest in You.

And, when feelings of disappointment try to crowd in, I will make that my warning signal, and I will stop and renew my choice to trust in You. Then Lord, the rest is up to You."

It is really as simple as that. You don't have to "feel" anything! This has to be an act of your will, not of your emotions. It has to be something you do on purpose, based on the promises God has clearly made, rather than something you do only if you happen to feel like it at the moment.

Disappointments Be Gone!

The Lord gave me a simple little statement to say out loud every time I am faced with an opportunity to be disappointed. I am simply to say, "Lord, in this particular situation (name the situation) I choose to trust You." I have probably repeated that one phrase more than 10,000 times. And quite frankly, I don't know what it is but there is something about saying it out loud that kicks the whole process into gear and releases the trust.

You won't necessarily be able to prevent certain thoughts from knocking at your mind's door, but you can control which thoughts you allow in and think through—fear and doubt thoughts and "what if " thoughts. Once you open up your mind's door to mull over the possibility that the Word might not work every time, out goes the trust and in comes the disappointment. And at that point the Rock (the Word) becomes a stumbling block.

√ **I am giving you life and death information today that can keep your spiritual walk from taking a big detour!** And I am not talking about positive thinking. I am talking about choosing to trust in God's Word to the extent that you develop an expectancy that God will do *exactly what He promises.*

√ **This is also not a passive trust or a "whatever will be will be" kind of trust!** This is a deep commitment that says, "Lord, I am trusting You in the middle of this impossible situation, and I know the time will come that I will not be disappointed— so *I am making the choice not to allow feelings of disappointment to overtake me now.*"

In the simplest possible terms you are activating an expectancy in—and a dependency on—God's integrity!

This is also not a mind over matter situation in which you refuse to think about your situation until it either goes away or gets better. You are not psyching yourself up; on the contrary, I am talking about a supernatural intervention. God says, "If you trust Me you will not be disappointed." God is big enough to work out any situation, no matter how impossible it looks. His Word tells us that He is the God of the impossible. But the degree to which we trust Him determines the degree of victory we will experience, because trust is basically the medium of exchange here.

You can't pay God but you can trust Him, and that's exactly what He wants you to do.

Now . . . there will be times when things don't look so good, when you can see no possibility that a given situation can ever work out right. Those are the times when you need to make it a determination—a challenge—to trust God without reservation, because at that moment you will either win or lose the battle. When trusting becomes a way of life, your life will become the most thrilling and exhilarating existence in the world. There is nothing more exciting than to constantly anticipate, in faith, how God is going to work out our impossible circumstances.

So . . . beginning with that one significant morning and throughout the next year, I awoke practically every morning and went to sleep almost every night quoting, "those who trust God will not be disappointed." It became a household phrase—a family motto. Little did we know that God was preparing us to learn how to walk in an exciting, peaceful state of victory we had never before known.

I am now going to share some of the stories of how God intervened in our lives in situation after situation, with this trust versus disappointment reality, while we were getting this foundational principle established within ourselves as individuals and within our family as a unit.

But first, I want to remind you of one secret that is paramount to everything else. There can be no real, lasting trust in God apart from a *love walk* with Him. Only to someone we have known and experienced personally can we ultimately release trust—someone with whom we have invested enough time to know intimately.

Thus says the Lord, "Cursed is the man who trusts in mankind and makes flesh his strength, and whose heart turns away from the Lord... Blessed is the man who trusts in the Lord and whose trust is the Lord." (Jeremiah 17:5,7)

The Miracles Begin

Back in 1977, Jack and I felt that the Lord was leading us to build a house in the country without going into debt. Instead, we were to look to Him continually to supply every need. This was a brand new adventure. I think our extended families thought we had lost our minds. But by the time the project was completed the experience had become such a training ground for us that the house itself had become like a fringe benefit.

Whether we'd built it or not, the truths we learned would have been worth all the work. Likewise with so many others we've talked to—we find that the things we experience can always be a training ground to grow spiritually, if we allow them to be. Only good gifts come from God, but He will take even the bad and turn it into good if we trust Him.

Lumber Galore

Our house was a large, full two-story with more than 3000 square feet in the downstairs alone, and since we were doing much of the construction work ourselves it took us three and a half years to complete it. It would not be an exaggeration to say that miracles happened at every step of the way.

When the initial plumbing and the enormous cement foundation slab were completed, we considered using metal for the framework but decided on wood when we heard that the old Swift Turkey Processing Plant had gone out of business and was auctioning off everything, including the lumber. Since Jack couldn't take off work to go to the auction, he sent my dad with a blank check to buy—if the quality of the lumber was good, and if he could get it for a good price.

Jack was a little nervous about sending my dad with a blank check because Dad was notorious for loving auctions, and he had bought some things in the past for which we still hadn't found a purpose.

We hadn't heard from Dad all day, so when Jack got off work that afternoon we made a beeline for the auction ground. The auction was over and the place was practically empty, and the only person we saw was my dad, standing in the middle of this huge lot, wiping beads of perspiration off his brow.

The first words out of Jack's mouth were, "Did you buy anything?" With one big sweep of the hand, Dad replied, "I bought all of this!"

Mounds of lumber—some stacks taller than a two story building—were piled all over the lot. I saw a look of horror cross Jack's face. It would take weeks to haul it all out to our building site, some ten miles in the country. But before he could voice that fear, Dad blurted out, "The lot has to be cleared in three days or they'll bulldoze it all under."

Sure enough, several big bulldozers were parked off to the side. The Kwik Pantry Convenience Store had purchased the land for a gas station, and they were on a tight schedule.

I called it "piles" because it was not stacks of lumber that had been cleaned of its nails and neatly stacked. Every board was filled with nails and they were all thrown up on gigantic piles. Dad was already frantically pulling boards off the pile and loading them on his pickup. He had spent the maximum amount that we had allotted, plus half again as much, and the reality of what we had facing us to get the lot cleared in time was just beginning to dawn on him. The boards were so long that we couldn't even get them in the pickup without extending them way over the cab and far too many feet out the back of the bed.

I could feel Jack's fear and disappointment mounting as he started to walk around those piles and pray. Talk about an impossible-looking task! The sight was mind-boggling, but we couldn't give up because all our money was tied up in that lumber. We had to salvage as much as possible.

A New Trailer Too!

In a few moments Jack called me over and said that God had told him to go to Santa Anna, a town twenty miles away, where he would find a harvest gold, sixteen-foot cattle trailer with a bulldog hitch, and it would cost under $1000.

Dad was not happy when we took off on what he thought was a wild goose chase, but like the colt on which Christ entered Jerusalem, the trailer was there exactly as God had said it would be. It took a couple of phone calls to hunt the owner down, but he sold it to us for just $975 because he was closing that particular brand out in order to carry a much more cheaply made line.

We spent every moment of daylight for the next three days, hauling lumber—trip after trip after trip! But praise God, even though we did not have one hour to spare, we were able to clear the lot before the bulldozers started leveling the ground for their new building.

For the next three months I stood outside under the trees on our own property, with two saw horses supporting the boards as, one by one, I pulled nails and dropped them into a #2 washtub. I counted one hundred twenty-two nails in one of those boards, and I think that was a pretty fair average. No wonder I was barely able to stay ahead of Jack and his partner as they started the framework on the house!

On the other hand, the carpenter who helped with the framework could not quit commenting on the quality of the lumber that came out of that old turkey processing plant. Over each of our windows and patio doors we were able to install full sized 2" x 14" headers, and we had enough tongue-in-groove oak to deck the entire second floor, making it solid as a rock.

By the time we were finished we had all the lumber we needed, plus enough extra for three other people who wanted to build on extra rooms and garages. God's provision always includes an abundance left over to help others.

> And God is able to make all grace abound to you,
> that always having all sufficiency in everything, you
> may have an abundance for every good deed.
> (2 Corinthians 9:8)

Our carpenter estimated that we had bought at least $8,000 worth of lumber—many times more than what we paid. And after using that cattle trailer for a number of years, we were able to sell it for more than we paid for it in the beginning.

Along with the lumber my dad also got two huge metal I-beams. Two men could not even begin to lift one end, but a house mover offered to haul them out to our house and even refused to accept any payment for the trip. Those I-beams made the best cattle guard in our part of the country, as proven over and over after everything from concrete trucks to loaded gravel trucks made numerous trips across, with not one bit of give showing up in the beams.

Inside and Outside Bricks

We knew we would need our bricks fairly early in the construction process because we were using them on the inside as load-bearing walls for the upstairs. But we weren't overly concerned, because three months before we started construction we were told at the local brick plant that they needed only a week's notice to have bricks for us.

We didn't think about how things can change! Now, almost a year later, it was time to put up the inside brick walls, so we scheduled the bricklayer to come the next week. Our big concern had been getting on his busy schedule, but with that all worked out we drove to the brick plant to place the brick order.

Distracted by our busy schedule, we had not paid attention to all the new construction going on around the state. Since our first visit with the manager at the brick yard there had been such a building boom that there were no bricks to be had at the local plant—or anywhere else in Texas! We were told that we would be put on the waiting list, but not to expect a call for at least six months.

We could have waited on the bricks for the outside of the house, but we had to have those bricks for the inside before we could get the house dried in. That kind of delay would have caused the wooden framework of the house to warp. So, in desperation we asked the manager of the brick plant if we could pay a premium price to get the bricks early. The moment those words came out of his mouth Jack knew he was wrong and wished he could have stuffed them back down his throat, but it was too late. The man very angrily let us know that he didn't take bribes or do business that way. Jack apologized and said that he didn't do business that way either.

Discouragement was running so high that neither of us spoke a word on the way home. To make matters in the natural seem even worse, when we got there we contacted a brick jobber who made phone calls to every brick company in Texas and even in the surrounding states, all to no avail.

Then, all of a sudden, both of us remembered the scripture that had formed the foundation for everything we'd done so far—*"Those who trust the Lord will not be disappointed."* Our own reasoning told us there were no possible answers, so it took everything we could do to choose not to be disappointed and to trust God to make a way.

Another Huge Shock

With all the strength we could muster, we began to confess that trust out loud. The next morning, after Jack's prayer time, he felt impressed to go back to the local brick company and apologize again. That seemed strange to me since he had apologized profusely the day before, but if that was going to make him feel any better, so be it. Jack was met with a cold shoulder when he first walked in, but as soon as he apologized again the man said, "I have your bricks." Jack said that he must have just stood there in shock for a full sixty seconds before he was able to utter a word.

Right after we left the brick plant the day before, a church in Waco, Texas, some 150 miles away, had called. After a year they still had their bricks on pallets waiting for an expansion project to begin. But now that they were finally ready to start, the committee decided that the bricks didn't match the existing building well enough, so they called the brick company to see if they could exchange them. They didn't mind paying extra, and they didn't mind the six-month wait if they could get what they wanted.

During that past year the brick company had quit producing that particular brick, so they offered them to us at last year's price if we would take them all. Sight unseen and without even knowing how many bricks we needed, we trusted that a miracle of this magnitude had to be from God, so we jumped at the offer. From the church in Waco to our doorstep, two truckloads of bricks were delivered the very next day. We didn't even have to reschedule our bricklayer.

They were not only the right color but they were also load-bearing bricks for supporting a second floor, something we had not even thought to ask about. We didn't have a clue how many bricks we needed for the walls, the columns, and the arches, but that was not even an issue after all the Lord had already done.

However, we weren't expecting it to be such an exact count. We had less than 300 bricks left over when we completed the project.

If a house had cancelled there wouldn't have been enough bricks, but we had exactly enough since they came from a larger project. God not only counts the hairs on our head, He even counts the number of bricks we need!

God is not wasteful, but His supply is always ample. If Jack had not heard his urging to go back to the brick company and apologize all over again the next day, the manager never would have thought of us. And even if he had, he didn't know our name and probably wouldn't have wanted to do us any favors if he had, considering what Jack had said the day before. All of which is a perfect example of how God can even use our mistakes to pull us out of our own woods!

Window Screens

With the house dried in and thirty-two windows installed (not counting the patio doors), we decided to store the window screens until the house was finished so they wouldn't get damaged during construction. Two and a half years later we finished the house and put the screens on the windows so we could move in.

Spring's arrival in the middle of a terrible Texas drought was a bad combination that year. Within a few weeks our light fixtures were swarming with bugs at night. I'm not talking about a few bugs that slip in when the doors are opened—the house was filled with bugs!

An investigation of the problem revealed holes in the plastic screens as big as softballs. We were horrified. What on earth could have happened? Well, it didn't take long to discover that the enormous grasshopper crop, with nothing else to eat, had gnawed on those plastic screens until they had made huge holes.

We had a lot of money tied up in all those screens, and the temptation to be disappointed was pretty overwhelming. Especially considering that those screens had been purchased more than two years before, putting them well outside the warranty period.

Even though they had been stored they were still considered "old screens," so there was not one thing we could do in the natural. We kept saying, "Lord, we don't know what can be done but we are going to trust You. And we choose not to allow feelings of disappointment to come in."

As Jack was leaving for work that morning he asked me to talk with the man at the lumber company. The manager listened to my story, took down the number and sizes of the windows, called the window company, briefly told them what had happened, and then added, "Keep in mind that they have had those windows for over two years." He didn't even bother to say that the screens had all been in storage.

The impression was exceptionally clear that he had made the call only to appease me, so for the next two weeks we contended with bugs. There was no air conditioning at the time, and we needed those windows for some breeze. So every time we contended with bugs and felt a wave of disappointment try to come over us, we made ourselves quote our scripture and confess our trust in the Lord, even though there was nothing whatsoever in the natural to give us any hope.

Two more weeks passed. Then one day I answered the phone and heard the voice on the other end of the line say, very simply, "We have your screens."

Even though it had been two and a half years, with no questions asked the supplier had made all new screens from screen wire rather than plastic and had shipped them free of charge. Once again, God had supernaturally intervened and we were not disappointed.

The Only Concrete in Town

We had intended to build a patio after the house was completed, but upon erecting the two-story wall in the den with no second floor over the den for support, we needed that patio immediately to shore up the wall and give it stability from the outside. A high wind on the hill where our house was being built could have played permanent havoc.

Right away Jack started building the cement forms for the patio foundation, only to be told that the concrete company could not promise a load of cement anytime in the near future. The building boom I mentioned earlier was still in full swing, making it very hard to get a concrete truck to come for a small pouring. There were so many large projects going on that the concrete company was working twenty-four hour shifts and still could not meet the demand.

Those are the times when listening to negative reports and looking at things in the natural will kill your faith and feed your disappointments. Being in constant remembrance that God is able to overcome the impossible is a must in order to stay in trust! I am not saying that your mind and emotions might not be screaming like those of the world, but we have to remind ourselves that we are, in reality, citizens of another world entirely.

When the concrete forms were completed, Jack called the cement company to place his order. He might have expected a refusal, but the refusal he got was not for the reasons he expected. The water canal from Lake Brownwood had collapsed during the night, and there was no water coming to Brownwood. Therefore, no concrete trucks were running.

Feeling impressed by God to place an order anyway, Jack had the dispatcher write it down, but the guy kidded him unmercifully for insisting when there was no water in the entire city of Brownwood. About midday, however, a temporary fix at the canal site turned the water back on. The water brought with it numerous orders for concrete, but since Jack's order had been the only one on the docket all morning, his was the first to be filled. And the moment Jack's order was filled, the canal immediately collapsed again and they were not able to get it repaired for the next couple of days, making our pour the only one in the county.

When it became known that ours was the only active construction site anywhere around, the men who finish out the concrete slabs followed the trucks to our place, giving Jack all the help he needed. Jack had already hired three, but seven extra men stayed and worked for nothing. When the job was done, rejoicing definitely took the place of any prior temptation to be disappointed!

Who Knows More About Construction?

A year before we started construction Jack was shown a radically different, new design concept that was supposed to better handle the weight of porches and balconies. As I said earlier we had nine eight-foot patio sliding glass doors throughout the house, upstairs and downstairs. But after being in the house less than two months we discovered that the patio doors would open only eight to ten inches, leaving hardly enough room to squeeze through. That was not a big concern, however, since the man who had installed the windows had suggested that they might need adjusting.

After working with the windows for a good while, however, he showed me where the heavy metal frames around the double-paned glass had already started bending. He had concluded that the house was settling and emphatically told me there was nothing that could be done. Eventually the pressure would break all the glass.

That house was built on a natural cliché gravel bed, and the foundation had been built stronger than building code. Yet the facts did seem obvious, and "by sight" we were in trouble. The words of the window installer kept ringing in my ears, and I got horror pictures in my mind of nine big holes in the walls where the patio doors had once been.

It seemed that throughout the construction we were taking turns reminding each other about our scripture promise, so once again we started confessing, "Lord, you gave us this scripture, and we have seen You come through many times before, so we are not going to give in to disappointment. We choose to trust You."

Several nights later Jack had a dream in which he saw himself jacking up the patio roof on the back of the house, as well as the balcony across the front. But when he called the man who had installed the patio doors to tell him what he intended to do, his excitement was very quickly dashed when the man told him that would put more pressure on the patio doors, which would only hasten the inevitable. Now Jack was faced with a dilemma— would he go with what man was saying or would he do what he believed God had shown him?

The next day we held our breath as he placed large house-moving jacks under the balcony and very carefully started levering it upward. Instead of putting more pressure on the glass as the man who had installed the doors anticipated, that new design concept lifted the pressure off the doors. And just as God had shown him in the dream, they began to open and close freely.

We are still thankful today for that new concept, because through all these years the balconies have never sagged. Every time I clean those patio doors and notice the bend in the frame I am reminded of God's faithfulness.

Purple Spots Galore

When it came time to think about carpet we thought we had met our Waterloo. We knew we were to pay as we went and avoid debt at all cost, but we needed five hundred yards of carpet. That seemed like a huge amount to me. I knew the kind of longwearing carpet I wanted, so I had been searching for almost a year. Just about the time I was ready to give up in defeat, a little carpet place went into business locally and decided to do us a favor. They ordered samples of discontinued carpet from a carpet mill in Georgia, assuring me that even though the carpet had been discontinued it was still top quality—not seconds.

When I got the samples, there it was—the exact carpet and color that I wanted—for precisely one-fifth the price I anticipated. I still have to look at the invoice from time to time to believe it!

So, about six months before it would be needed, four big rolls of carpet covered in white protective canvas were delivered to our door. Of course, I couldn't open a roll because of all the construction debris, but I pulled back the canvas just far enough to see that they had sent the right carpet. It was even more beautiful than I had remembered, although I was still puzzled that they had sent five hundred fifty yards instead of the five hundred we had ordered.

Months later the big day finally came for us to lay the carpet, and Jack insisted that we hire a Christian father-son team, even though we didn't know them personally and their bid was a good bit higher than the rest. Outside work allowed us to give them free run of the house, and I had determined not to even take a peek inside until it was finished. Excitement was running high, so you can imagine how I could think they were kidding with me when one of them came out to say, "Did you know that the carpet has big purple spots in it?" One look at the exposed roll of carpet in the large den floor let me know, however, that he was not joking.

I remember biting down hard on my lower lip to hold back the tears. He must have seen my panic because he quickly assured me that I didn't have anything to worry about—the carpet mill would have no dispute about replacing the defective merchandise.

Who But God…?

What he didn't know was that during the last six months the local carpet company had gone out of business, and the owners had moved out of town, leaving no forwarding address. There was also no name of the carpet mill from which the carpet had been purchased! We had the carpet—they had their money—and we never expected a problem!

All Jack could think of to do was to tell the two carpet layers to come back the next day, and we would come up with a plan. We started quoting, through tears at first, "Lord, I refuse to quit trusting you. I don't care how hopeless this situation appears to be; You have promised that we will not be disappointed if we trust You."

I had secretly expected the men not to return, but bright and early the next morning, there they were. Jack simply said, "I am trusting that God will give you an answer to this dilemma." It had become obvious why God had impressed us to get the Christian team, even though they had submitted a higher bid. Instead of walking out they took the challenge, and after an hour of serious deliberation they started measuring every square inch of the house.

Out of the four rolls of carpet, one roll had to be flawless for their plan to work. Laying out the measurements of halls, stairs, rooms, and closets on the carpet, much like you would lay pattern pieces on a piece of sewing material, they shifted them back and forth until the pieces miraculously avoided all the purple spots. But as they opened each new roll of carpet and found to it be full of those dreaded spots, anxiety mounted. Remembering that we had to have one perfect roll for the large den area, I don't think any one of us was breathing as the fourth roll was being uncurled.

When that last roll turned out to be flawless, it was several minutes before anyone in the room said a word. We were all speechless! Then everyone in unison, including the carpet layers, let out a shout that I'm sure you could have heard a mile down the road. It took all five hundred fifty yards of carpet! The five hundred yards we ordered would not have been enough. God is an awesome God!

There were times when sight was so strong in the negative that it was like pulling flesh off our bones to steadfastly determine—Lord, I am trusting you, and I will not be disappointed. Our minds were screaming, "Lord, how can this work out?" But that is really none of our business. Working things out is God's department. Our part is to choose to trust Him, correct ourselves at any point of obedience, and refuse to allow disappointment to sneak in the door. His part is bringing a solution to pass, and we were never able to guess how He was going to do it. But the one thing we could count on was that the trusting had to come first every single time.

That *"shall not be disappointed"* statement is literal! He is not saying that He will just dull the pain or make us forget the anguish. He is saying that He will intervene in our behalf with a miracle, if we will trust Him.

We kept a diary every day, because with each new opportunity to be disappointed the newest challenge always looked bigger than the last one. And when you are in the battle, it's easy to grow weary and want to throw in the towel. How quick we are to think, "Oh, my God, what now?"

With our human nature comes a tendency to forget past miracles when a new challenge arises. Those were the times when we would get out the diary and encourage our faith as we recounted miracle after miracle.

When negative thoughts are bombarding the mind, it is more important than ever to run to God in trust and not away from Him in disappointment. When we did steadfastly trust, *future tense*, we were never disappointed. Sometimes we had to wait a few hours, sometimes a few months, and sometimes a few years. But the answers always came.

Writing A Covenant As A Family

When we began building the house, we wrote up a covenant in which we all agreed to seek God for what He wanted to do in that project. Remembering the four of us—Jack, Angelia, Bill, and I, sitting around our table in the old house in town, praying together and writing that covenant—brings back one of my most special memories. In fact, I still have that original covenant, decades later, framed and hanging on the wall as a reminder of God's faithfulness. Little did I know how significant that covenant was going to be.

As we were praying together, with each one of us suggesting things that needed to be included in the covenant, someone said that he felt God wanted us to include the statement *"free telephone installation and a private line when needed."* None of us thought much about that at the time. We were still living in town, so neither telephone service nor a private line sounded like a problem. But when the time came to move to the new house in the country, we realized what we were up against in the natural.

Our nearest neighbor at that time was several miles closer to town than we were. In fact, he could see the telephone pole from his house yet it still cost several thousand dollars to have the line run from the pole to his home. At that rate it would cost us close to $10,000 for a phone!

The disappointing thought of not even being able to have a phone at all began to bombard all of our minds, so once again we had to make the conscious decision to trust God. Even though it looked impossible, we had seen God go beyond the impossible time and again.

Even so, I could not help thinking about the part of our covenant that had addressed the telephone issue directly. Had God known this would be such a predicament that we would have to confess our faith in Him for almost four years to break through? Whatever the case, I could see no possible answer.

An Amazing Contact

The next week Jack felt that we were to contact the telephone company and talk to a man by the name of Artie Ben Steele. We knew that he worked for the GTE Company, but we didn't know in what capacity and we didn't really know him personally. So, I called the telephone company and asked to speak to Mr. Steele, explaining that we had built a house and needed a phone installation.

They very quickly told me that Mr. Steele didn't have anything to do with residential telephone installations, and that I needed to just write a letter, asking for someone to come out and give us an estimate for the hookup.

In the telephone conversation I never even gave my name, and I certainly didn't mention that there were no telephone lines within several miles of the house. I just wrote the letter requesting a telephone line. Deciding that Jack must have missed

God in what he thought he heard, I deliberately did not mention Mr. Steele's name in the letter.

A few days later we got a response through the mail. But in addition to the letter itself there was a personal note attached, saying, "I took the liberty of taking your letter out of 'such-and-such' department. We have an underground telephone cable project that is almost complete between Brownwood and Indian Creek, and you are in the direct line. If you would like to be a part of that project, let us know."

The enclosed letter then explained that we would be given free telephone installation, and that we could have a private line if we wanted one. Those were the very words that we had put in our covenant! I was already screaming with excitement, but I lost my voice entirely when I finished the letter and saw that it was signed by . . . Artie Ben Steele. Coincidence? Not on your life!

GTE

GENERAL TELEPHONE COMPANY OF THE SOUTHWEST
P. O. Box 996
Brownwood, Texas 76801

Teleph
(915) 643

September 16, 1977

Mr. Jack Ruth
1003 LaMonte
Brownwood, Texas 76801

During the second quarter of 1978, we will be placing new telephone
facilities in your area. Applicants that apply now for service can
be included in the project and served without an aid-to-construction
charge. We can provide one-party, four-party or eight-party service
to you when the project is completed. There would be the standard
installation charge when service is established.

The monthly rates for the following types of basic telephone service
(excluding extensions and premium type instruments) at your present
location in the Brookesmith-Indian Creek area would be:

One-party residence service	$21.00—includes mileage charge of $12.00
Four-party residence service	12.10
Eight-party residence service	9.65

Please advise by September 22, 1977, the type of service you desire
if you want to be included in the project.

If you have any questions, please call 643-1621 and indicate that you
have questions concerning the Indian Creek-Brookesmith survey and the
receptionist will transfer you to someone that can assist you.

Your reply to this letter will be appreciated.

A. B. Steele
A. B. STEELE
Business Office Supervisor

Provisions in Abundance

As soon as we got moved in, different people began offering us things for the house. We had never had people outside the family just call to give us something, yet suddenly, it was like the sky just opened up.

√   One lady gave me an old, beautifully refinished player piano.

√   My friend, Brenda, had just ordered new custom-made drapes and a king-sized bedspread with matching wallpaper when a fire broke out in her kitchen and caused smoke damage throughout the house. The insurance company paid to completely remodel the inside of the entire house, and since the new drapes and bedspread would no longer match the remodeling job she gave me the wallpaper (still on the rolls), the border paper, and the custom-made drapes and bedspread. Angelia was delighted with a room that looked like it came straight out of a *House Beautiful* magazine.

√   A visiting friend from California saw the large, empty, thousand square-foot family room and told us that God had impressed her to give us a massive sectional couch that she no longer had a room big enough to accommodate. However, getting the couch from California was going to be such a huge financial expenditure that I couldn't get excited about it until my sister said that she and her husband were taking a trip to California that weekend and would be happy to bring it back in a U-haul. From the moment I laid eyes on that custom made, Spanish couch, I knew it had been especially designed for our den.

√   A lighting company went out of business and we were able to get Spanish light fixtures for the entire house at a fraction of the normal cost. We actually wired the house to fit those elaborate fixtures.

√   When it came time to put the cover plates on the electrical plugs and switches, we felt impressed one morning to go to one of the lumberyards. In front of the building was a huge, flatbed truck with stacks of the very heavy metal Amerock cover plates that I had wanted—along with enough metal door knobs of the same color and design for every inside and outside door, plus hinges and drawer pulls. There were only three bathroom towel racks, three toothbrush holders and three toilet tissue holders—one for each of our three bathrooms! Everything was on sale for half price, but when we offered to buy it all we got it for fifteen cents on the dollar.

As our project came to a close we knew exactly what God had meant when He said that the building of the house would be such a learning experience in trust that the house itself would be like a fringe benefit. Rather than serving a God who teaches His children obedience by sending tragedy, we serve an awesome God who loves to teach us His kind ways through His abundant blessings.

The diary I had been keeping became invaluable. I knew the time would come when I would have a hard time remembering—and even believing—some of these miracles, if they had not been recorded regularly as they happened. Each provision had been unique and so overwhelmingly amazing.

Our Covenant

Dear Heavenly Father:

On this day of November 30, 1976, we stand on the promises of Your word, and we commit to You our new home located on Your land to be used to glorify Your Son. We agree according to your Word (Phil 4:19) that You will give us exact instructions on a daily basis and that all the supplies, money, patience, and wisdom will be supplied on time from Your Holy Spirit. Free telephone installation and private line will be made available when needed. This Casa de Paz will have both happiness, joy, peace and blessings with total protection. (Psalm 91) Lord, we agree that You will be merciful and loving as You teach us to depend on You daily. There will be peace continually. We agree in the Name of Jesus that this home will be completed soon enough for the entire family to enjoy its benefits, and it will strengthen the love in our family. The workmen that you choose will be available as needed. All furnishings, material, and workmanship will be perfect, chosen by You and without blemish. The interior and exterior and landscaping will be beautifully coordinated by You with comfort and uniqueness showing forth Your glory.

We bind satan & any demonic spirits—especially discouragement, doubts, fear, confusion, and reasoning—from any interference or harassment. The house will be debt-free financially and from any other obligation, except love. Our home in Brownwood will be sold at the right price, to the right buyer and at the right time. All members of the family will be praising you for a perfect gift. Kingdom living will reign continually at this site, and total freedom will result for all concerned. All glory, honor, & praise be to the Lord.

Your Word says where two or more agree on anything in the Name of Jesus, it shall be done. Lord, we put You in remembrance of Your Word, and we call your attention, satan, to our agreement with our Father.

Amen & so let it be,

Jack, Peggy Joyce, Angelia, Bill

Where You Lead Me I Will Follow

Busy was hardly the word for those house-building years. It felt as though Jack were living three lives, but actually it was more like living three shifts.

√ He was doing shift work forty hours a week at 3M, plus overtime.

√ He was building on the house another forty hours a week, or more.

√ He was ministering to a steady stream of people who found their way to our door during those years.

Evidently God was preparing Jack for the pastorate, because even as the house was taking shape on the inside, God was already filling it with people from the outside who needed help. We had prayed that every single person who set foot in the family room would be saved, healed, and delivered, and God evidently took that prayer seriously, judging by how many lives were set free during those years.

As in the case of the loaves and fishes, it takes so little from us for God to do so much with it. We still hear reports, years later, from people we had forgotten who were ministered to during that era. One dramatic case will probably always stand out in our minds.

Late one night we opened the door to find a young man from out of town, who had brought his wife at gunpoint for ministry. Even though a warrant for his arrest for kidnapping her had been sworn out, no one would have thought to look for him at our house. So Jack had plenty of time to deal with the situation. And, as the evening progressed and the nervousness subsided, God did some miraculous things.

The young man, who thought that only his wife needed help, was amazingly set free that night. He was even willing, afterwards, for Jack to take him to the police station where all the charges were dropped. Meanwhile, his wife received some much-needed inner healing. Then God put the icing on the cake. After the trauma that their marriage had been put through, who would have believed it still could have been salvaged? But God did the impossible and it is still intact today.

As we took care of God's business, God was faithful to take care of the needs and potential disappointments in our life. And some of God's protection from disappointment during those years came through acts of obedience on our part. Those subtle little nudges that are easy to overlook can sometimes make all the difference.

The Lord Saw It Coming

For example, one morning Jack came out from under the kitchen sink, where he'd been putting in the plumbing, to tell me that God had impressed him to go into town and buy plumbing supplies and a long garden hose to connect inside the hot water heater closet to use in case of fire. I, of course, wanted him to finish the sink plumbing before he started another project, but he was determined. It was late afternoon, after the fire hose was installed, before he got back to plumbing the sink.

Meanwhile, for weeks we had been piling limbs and brush to burn on the first perfectly calm day. We are on a hill and windless days are rare, but late on that same afternoon, after Jack had installed the fire hose, the breeze died down and Bill asked to burn the pile of brush that had now grown as tall as the second floor.

Unfortunately, the scraps of Masonite boards that Bill and I had been piling on the stack were not visible under all those tree limbs, so Jack gave him the okay. Bill and I found out the hard way that Masonite burns unusually hot and keeps a fire going for a long time.

As the mound reached full blaze, the wind suddenly kicked up and started blowing unusually hard. A deafening roar brought all of us out of the house to find that what should have been a safely contained brush fire, which would have burned out quickly, was now a huge mass of unbelievably hot flames being blown straight toward the house. One tree had already been engulfed, and we knew it would be only a matter of time until the others would be ignited. These were the days before cell phones and before our telephone had been installed.

Jack didn't have time to investigate to find out what had gone wrong. He dashed to the water heater closet, unrolled the long water hose that he had just installed, and kept the water blasting full-force on the trees that would have otherwise ushered the fire right up to the house. Three hours later we were finally satisfied that things were completely under control and it was okay to turn the water hose off. The only things damaged were a few of the trees that were alarmingly close to the house.

Even some of the neighbors from three miles down the road, seeing the blaze and thinking it was the house, had come to help. I have often wondered what would have happened if Jack had not been obedient and had not stopped his sink plumbing and gone immediately to plumb in the water hose. It was worth its weight in gold on that one occasion.

Custom-Made Cabinets

Jack had never built cabinets and got a little nervous whenever he thought about a huge houseful of cabinets yet to be built. But driving home one afternoon, he felt impressed to stop and walk through a new home that was under construction. He was surprised to find an old carpenter busily working after hours on the cabinets. When he heard about the task Jack had in front of him he sat down and spent the next couple of hours drawing designs and explaining in detail how to bring them to reality. No one would believe my cabinets were the first ones Jack ever built.

Blessings in Unexpected Places

By the time we were ready to move in we lacked only a few pieces of furniture—a large foyer table for the entrance hall, a small piece of furniture to hold napkins for the dining room, a coffee table for the upstairs sitting area, and a few lamp tables.

On an out-of-town trip to Rockport and Corpus Christi we found ourselves with a few hours to fill, so we drove through one of the nicer sections of town to look at the new homes. When I discovered that one of the large houses was advertising an inside garage sale, I couldn't resist the opportunity to see the interior of that lovely home—having no idea that it was a God appointment.

The lady told me that the sale was actually over and she had only a few odds and ends of Spanish furniture left, but I was welcome to look. I stood there speechless when I walked in. There was my beautiful foyer table, a small piece of furniture that she said had no purpose (but was perfect for my napkin collection), a large coffee table, lamp tables, and a bookcase as an added bonus—which, by the way, gave me just what I needed on an empty wall in the upstairs reading room.

Every single item I had needed or wanted was there, plus one. And because the sale was over and we were willing to take everything she had left, she practically gave the furniture away. I might add that if anything had been an inch larger in any direction, we would not have been able to get it all in the Suburban, but it fit perfectly. Because, before we left home Jack had felt impressed to take the seats out of the back of the car!

One Step at a Time

S ometimes God's answers come in progressive steps. I think it's those times—when the situation seems to go from bad to worse, even though He's working things out in the background—that challenge us the most to stand firm in faith and continue to trust.

A Miracle on Four Legs

Bill, of course, is grown now, but when he was in his teens he started praying and believing God for a horse. Jack and I tried to discourage him because we didn't want him to be disappointed, but he insisted that God had told him that he would be given a palomino horse that enjoyed being ridden, and that someone would come to know the Lord because of the horse. Skepticism ran a little high in both Jack and me when Bill claimed that the horse would also be an evangelistic tool. It sounded rather manipulative, but it turned out to be quite true.

Somehow God worked it out so that a Christian racehorse breeder in Del Rio, who lived three hundred miles away and who was completely unknown to us, heard about the young man in Brownwood who was believing God for a horse. This horse breeder decided to give Bill a horse as a seed faith offering for something he was believing God for, and he even delivered the horse as he came through Central Texas on his way to Oklahoma. Only Jack and I knew the details that Bill believed God had given him about the mare, so when she arrived Bill was the only one who was not surprised to find that she was a beautiful palomino.

And as you would expect, at the very next church service Bill stood up and told everyone about his blessing from God—and that he had named her "Faith."

What I didn't expect was the call I got early the next morning from the mother of a fifteen-year-old girl who was visiting in the church service for the first time when Bill gave his testimony. The mother explained that the father was a new psychiatrist in Brownwood, a confessed agnostic who had so much influence on the girl's life that she had never been interested in the Lord before.

Out of boredom the girl had gone to church with her mother the night when she heard Bill's testimony. On the way home she had told her mother, "I can believe in a God like that. He's real!" Kim accepted the Lord and became one of our most faithful members until her family moved out of town.

(Just as a side note: After the Sunday morning service about two months ago I had a young woman come up and grab me around the neck. It was Kim, excited to introduce her husband and two small children and let me know that she was still going with God. I praise God for His keeping power!)

But back to my story! Two of the three things that Bill had thought God told him had come to pass. Someone had, in fact, come to know Jesus because of the horse (in spite of our skepticism), and Faith was a beautiful palomino. But the mare did not like to be ridden at all! Lord, why? It wouldn't have been any harder to give Bill a horse that liked to be ridden—would it?!

Faith Fights Back

Faith would do anything in her power to get the rider off her back. Standing straight up on her hind legs and doing a little dance until she dislodged her excess baggage was one of her favorite tricks. At other times she would take off like a streak of lightning, hoping to encourage her frightened passenger to bail off. Confusion filled my mind as I felt pulled between fighting thoughts of disappointment and, on the other hand, remembering the miraculous way in which she had been given to Bill. The straw that broke the camel's back came on the afternoon when one visitor, even though she had been warned, couldn't resist the temptation to try out her riding skills. She stayed on longer than most, but came out of the saddle just as Faith rounded a corner in the pasture, throwing her head first into a huge corner fence post. One frightening night in the hospital later the girl was okay, but all we could think of after that was trying to talk Bill into selling the mare.

In spite of the no horse-riding rule, Bill steadfastly refused to give up his prized possession from God. She made a nice, gentle pet as long as you weren't on her back, but the fact still remained that God had told him that he would be given a horse that liked to be ridden.

One day Bill came in to tell us that God had told him to have the mare bred. My first thoughts were, "Oh, no, more problems!" Instead, once we'd gone ahead it quickly became obvious that the new colt was the horse that God had been planning for Bill. That colt, Jim Dandy, loved Bill from the moment he was born. When it came time to saddle break him for riding, Jim Dandy never even attempted to buck—not even once.

Years later, when Bill would come home from college, after months of Jim Dandy's not being ridden, Bill could throw on a saddle and ride him all over the pastures as though they had never missed a day. Every time I would see them dashing through the fields together, tears would fill my eyes and all I could say was, "Lord, You are so good!"

Truly the time came that we were not disappointed! But as I said, sometimes God's answers do come in progressive steps, and we have to keep our trust and our faithfulness on Him during that interim period when it can feel as if we're groping through a dark tunnel. But if we keep trusting, His Light will always shine through when He knows the timing is right.

Gaining by Losing

When I think of trusting God through a series of circumstances, I always think of this particular situation. After Jack's dad went on to be with the Lord, Jack sold a business that they owned together. Never having been without a job before,

Jack got in too big a hurry and took a job with a rotating shift because he couldn't stand being without work.

That rotating shift, especially the night shift, kept him feeling like he was in continuous jet lag, so for three years he prayed for God to deliver him from the revolving schedule. Finally, a good position opened up in management and the selection process was quickly narrowed down to Jack and one other employee. Jack was much better qualified because of his experience in management, but the other applicant got the job even though he really didn't have several of the qualifications required for the position.

Finding out that the guy who got the position was a drinking buddy with the assistant plant manager didn't make us feel any better about the whole thing. I can promise you that it was a big temptation to think, "Lord, you let us down. Here we are trying to live for You, and this guy, who is obviously not living for You, gets the job."

For months that night shift got harder and harder, and Jack kept saying, "Lord, I'm trusting You and I refuse to allow myself to get into disappointment, but it is tempting to ask—why?!"

But then, during this interim period a new FMC company came to Brownwood. Jack applied and was one of the first to be hired. It was a better position, better pay, and best of all— daytime hours.

Three months later the first company had a layoff and closed a department, leaving the guy who'd been given the first shift job out walking the street after seventeen years with the company. Had Jack been put into that first shift position he would have been caught in the layoff, and he also would have missed the job with the new company because of the time overlap. God knows the future! He knows not only what's best for us today, but He also knows what will be the best for us all the way to the end.

Much of life is a progressive journey in which we can't always see around every corner, but God can. We absolutely cannot lose if we'll trust—and *continue* to trust—in God's faithfulness to us. Trust is a confident hope—a literal *expectation*—in God's faithfulness, and the Bible promises that the God kind of hope will not disappoint.

> *Hope does not disappoint, because the love*
> *of God has been poured out within our hearts*
> *through the Holy Spirit who was given to us.*
> *(Romans 5:5)*

I am convinced, however, that we can negate the Word and never receive the promise that was intended, if we allow disappointment to rob us of our trust and our hope in His faithfulness. Temptations will come, but if we embrace disappointment and become bitter we will miss out, and the Rock will become to us a Rock of stumbling.

Don't Negate the Promise

Let me give you a prime example of negating the promise. Years ago Angelia was getting ready to go to the Philippines as a summer missionary with an Oral Roberts University team. Each team member was required to raise his own money. Tim was especially excited about the trip because, being the only team member with a Master's degree, he had been asked to speak at the Bible College in Manila.

The whole team had worked hard to get their money together, but when the first deadline came and Tim's money wasn't in place, disappointment and bitterness caused him to start saying, "Oh, well, I didn't really want to go anyway." Other team members kept trying to keep him encouraged, reminding him that God could still do a last-minute miracle, but he dogmatically hung onto his disappointment in a God that he thought had let him down.

School ended and the team members started home to pack for the trip. No sooner had Angelia arrived than someone from our community called to say that God had laid it on her heart that there was someone on the team without finances to go, and she was to pay his way.

There was no question, whatsoever, that the person was Tim, so Angelia called the Mission Department to have them contact the young man. To her surprise, however, they refused, saying that his attitude was not what they wanted on a mission team. All of her reasoning with them, and explaining that he had simply reacted out of disappointment, was not enough to change their opinion—so Tim never knew about the provision.

I think about that often! It was a classic case of disappointment coming between a person and God's blessing. The money was there but Tim never knew God was faithful. He will probably go through life thinking that God failed him when, in reality, he quit trusting and allowed disappointment to come in. And the Word became to him a *rock of stumbling* and a *rock of offense*.

I have wondered how often I've lost the blessing because I laid down my trust and picked up disappointment, thinking that it was God who had failed me. I am convinced that if we get disappointed and stay there, letting bitterness take root, we will tie up the situation in the spiritual realm until the victory is lost.

Angelia on mission trip in Philippines praying for a sick baby

Some Say It's Too Late!

What about those times when something seems to have already been stolen? Don't forget that we serve a big God who promises that, if we trust Him and love Him, He will still work it all together for good.

> *And we know that God causes all things to work together for good to those who love God ,to those who are called according to His purpose...*
>
> *(Romans 8:28)*

Our car was stolen out from under our carport and we had no theft insurance. With everyone thinking it was too late, including the Sheriff Department, this was a real temptation to be disappointed. It was a fact that the car was gone, and after two weeks the officers insisted that it was already in Mexico.

Serious thefts were going on all around us— saddles, horses, horse trailers . . . we had all kinds of emotions to contend with, especially the fear that came from thinking, "If this could happen to us, what else could happen?" But fears, human reasoning, and thoughts of doubt have to be stopped because they always open the door to disappointment.

I can remember the night that Jack and I discussed the situation and finally came to the conclusion that there can be no "What ifs?" with the Lord. We determined that night that even though it looked to be too late, we were going to trust God to work it out. We prayed and asked God to forgive and convict whoever had taken the car, and we chose to forgive them according to the Word.

If you forgive the sins of any, their
sins have been forgiven them; if you retain
the sins of any, they have been retained.

(John 20:23)

One week later a young man turned himself in, saying that he had stolen a car and a company pickup. He was brought to our house where he confessed to us, "I've stolen all my life, but this is the first time I have ever felt guilty."

He couldn't remember exactly where he had left our car since he was stumbling drunk that night, but he did recall that it was left on a rodeo grounds. After some investigating we found that a little community called Elm Grove, located about fifteen miles from Brownwood, had sponsored a rodeo a couple of weekends before. And sure enough, there on the grounds was our '64 black Chevrolet Impala Sports Coupe, without a dent or a scratch on it. The only difference we could find was that it had a full tank of gas in place of its almost empty tank when it was taken!

The time came that we weren't disappointed but the temptation had certainly been there, because it appeared to have been too late. It is worth anything it takes to ignore negative feelings, to refuse to entertain fear over what appears to be obvious and to choose not to be disappointed.

God Brought It Back Again

We have had several occasions when it appeared to be too late. Several years ago we made an investment with a supposedly reputable investment company in Florida and lost the entire several-thousand dollar investment. The temptation to be disappointed was even stronger when we began to suspect that the broker had been dishonest, but we couldn't prove a thing.

Jack kept refusing to get into disappointment, and finally one day, out of the clear blue sky, the Lord impressed Bill to write to the Better Business Bureau. Two years later we got a check through the mail, refunding the entire amount. Everyone says that it is impossible in the natural to get 100% refunded without any court procedures, especially from just a letter—but praise God, it is not impossible with Him.

Who Can Command the Weather?

When Angelia and David married we had the wedding and the dinner at our house on July 30, 1988. That particular year came during the height of the drought, and always in Texas the end of July brings some of the hottest days of the entire year— usually well over one hundred degrees. We were dreading the heat and had prayed a lot about that.

Friends of mine were helping to decorate and coordinate the dinner outside on the lawn for more than three hundred guests. As I said, this happened before the drought broke, and we couldn't remember a time in years when it had rained in July. In fact, rain that time of year was such a "perceived impossibility" that we had not even thought to pray about it.

So you can imagine how shocked we were when, on July 30th, the darkest storm you can imagine began to build in the early afternoon. I remember looking out the upstairs' window at the round tables with beautiful floor-length, pink linen tablecloths arranged in a semicircle. The large baskets of flowers on each table were being blown off and down the hill faster than the ladies could pick them up.

The sky was black. I'm not talking about a summer shower; I'm talking about a thunderstorm. The trees were filled with twinkly lights, and it looked as though the wind was going to blow them completely out of the branches.

In addition to that crisis, we had not heard a word from the band that was supposed to have been at the house by two pm. The photographer, who was to fly over and take aerial pictures, had said, "I must have a perfectly clear day with no wind to get any good shots." It was now four-thirty and the wedding would start at seven pm.

I cannot tell you the mental pictures that were flashing through my mind. I imagined guests drenched to the skin. Or worse yet, no guests at all. Since the dinner was already prepared for over three hundred guests to be served outside, where would I serve them if they did show up? In my wildest imagination I could not think of a solution.

Everyone kept running in and asking, "What do we do?"—as if I knew! Finally Jack and I closed ourselves up in the bedroom and prayed, "Lord, this is our biggest challenge up to this time. What do we do?" I had poured myself into that wedding for the past seven months, and giving in to disappointment and anger would have been the easiest thing in the world to do, but it calmed my emotions when I heard Jack say, "Lord, in this particular situation—our daughter's wedding—we choose to trust You."

No Time for a Nap!

Having made that decision verbally, Jack lay down to take a nap. With all the upheaval that was going on I was so shocked that I just said, "What are you doing?"—to which he calmly replied, "If we are trusting God to take care of things, I want to feel good enough to enjoy the party." My husband is something else! He never ceases to amaze me.

From four-thirty until six the sky stayed so black that it looked as though it would open up and flood. The wind was so terrible that the ladies had long since brought all the tablecloths and flowers inside. But right before the guests began to come at six, the storm just suddenly went around us. Within minutes the band from San Antonio drove up. They had been lost for the last two and a half hours! And it didn't even sprinkle to mess up the grass.

By about eight o'clock, as the guests came out of the house to be seated for dinner after the wedding ceremony, the storm had gone exactly west of us. The tables were on a hill overlooking a valley to the west, and the sun setting behind those storm clouds was absolutely the most beautiful sight I had ever seen.

The very rain clouds that had threatened disaster created a breathtaking sunset. I don't think we have ever had one as beautiful since. The guests could hardly eat their dinner for talking about it and jumping up to take pictures of it. Perhaps more pictures were taken of the sunset than of the bride and groom!

It was almost as if God had written His blessing in the sky. I know how Noah must have felt when he saw that rainbow. That sunset was definitely a perfect reminder that those who trust the Lord will not be disappointed, even when we can't see a solution.

The storm had also blown away the mosquitoes and had cooled everything down into the mid-seventies. On July 30th that is nothing short of a miracle. I just kept brushing back the tears that night, with everyone thinking, of course, that it was because my daughter was getting married. In reality, the tears were because I could hardly contain the gratitude and excitement I felt in my heart toward God, for His goodness and for this wonderful scripture promise!

This is such a simple answer, but God's answers are so simple. This is one of the most important and life-changing truths you will ever hear. I believe that is why it is in the Word so many times. It works!

Will Our Children Miss Out?

You might have noticed, in our covenant, that we had said, "We agree in the Name of Jesus that this home will be completed soon enough for the entire family to enjoy its benefits." One of my biggest opportunities to be disappointed lay half-buried in the three and a half years it took to complete the house, so that by the time we were ready to move in Angelia was in her senior year of high school and Bill was close behind. Why had God told us to build a house of that size when the children would not be around to enjoy it?

As many miracles as God had already wrought, you would think that this particular fear would not have fazed me, but just as the Bible tells us, "the little foxes spoil the vine."

I don't think either child was hurt by this, and my anxieties at that time sound even more absurd as I talk about them now, but it all felt like a huge issue at the time. Jack talked me through it by reminding me that our children would certainly not be damaged from a project God had prearranged, and I knew in my heart he was right.

Even before Angelia and Bill left for college there was a constant flow of ministry that began pouring through the house—counseling, retreats, parties, seminars—plus, every Wednesday night, seventy-five to a hundred people came for mid-week Bible study and the popcorn fellowship that followed. I comforted myself by realizing that God had indeed arranged for the "entire family" to enjoy the house— the entire *church* family, that is!

But when God says that you won't be disappointed, He means literally, wholeheartedly, that you won't be disappointed. After college, Angelia and David moved to Dallas where David worked on his doctorate in Chiropractics, followed by an internship at one of the leading chiropractor clinics.

Much to everyone's surprise, a chain of events led them back to Brownwood to open a clinic here. But the high cost of buying equipment, remodeling a building, and establishing a clientele left them with few choices other than moving in with us for a while. They occupied the upstairs, enjoying the house in ways that Angelia never would have appreciated as a teenager. Their busy schedule kept them on the go, with hot meals waiting for them when they did make it home. And being the socialites that they are, they had a place big enough to entertain guests as often as they liked. Also, Jack and I got to be a part of their lives in ways that most parents of married children never have the opportunity to experience. What a beautiful and unique way the Lord has of fulfilling His promises.

By this time Bill had graduated from law school in Houston, Sloan had just given birth to their precious little boy, Cullen, and Bill had just enough experience to know that working for a big city law firm might not be what God had in mind for him. Beyond that, a combination of several things helped them decide that they wanted to raise their child in a small town—so they, too, moved back to Brownwood.

Bill had teased Angelia about moving back home with mom and dad, saying that big bird had returned to the nest. Now, facing the reality of starting a law practice from scratch and having a family to provide for, moving back home for a time did not sound like such a bad idea. It was even worth having to endure Angelia's teasing about "little bird kicking big bird out of the nest to make room for little bird to come back again."

not only did Bill move back, he brought pets

At last, in this area that had so forcefully threatened my peace when they had left home after high school, the promise of not being disappointed had reached its fulfillment. Both Jack and I, together with our children and their spouses, have been able to enjoy our home in ways that have far exceeded my fondest expectations. God is so awesome and so matchless. Who can anticipate how He will carry out His promises? He just never runs out of His amazing ways and means!

PJ & Sloan enjoying Mother's Day breakfast in bed

Egg on My Face

I want to share one final example that is simply too humorous to leave out, even though it makes me look really bad. Back during the time when Jack was between jobs and we were building on the house, money was extremely tight so I decided that until we got through the crisis I wouldn't replace anything I ran out of unless it was really a necessity. So right away I ran out of vanilla . . . but I could certainly do without that!

Several weeks went by, and I started making this special cake for a church luncheon, forgetting that this particular cake does not taste good without the right flavoring. I lived about ten miles out in the country, had no close neighbors to borrow from, and didn't have my car that day.

I'm embarrassed to tell you that I sat down on the floor and for a few minutes had my own little pity party, "Lord, this is really abundant living! I don't even have any vanilla to make this cake!" I think God must have allowed me to hear myself, because instantly I realized how ridiculous I was acting. So, I genuinely repented and started thanking God for all my blessings.

The next week I was helping some friends move from a large house into a mobile home in which they would be living for the summer while they went to school. I was carrying small items up the stairs into the mobile home when my friend, who was right behind me, said, "Oh, by the way, could you use any vanilla?" I stopped still in my tracks! Only the Lord knew about my little pity party the week before, and it was almost as if He had told on me.

As I turned around she shoved a large shoe box into my hands that was packed full of bottles of vanilla and every other kind of flavoring you could imagine. I just stood there speechless. It was as if the Lord were saying, "Do you think that will be enough vanilla for you?" The Lord definitely has a sense of humor. I could almost see Him smiling.

More than that, it also felt like He was saying, "I clothe the hills better than Solomon himself was dressed. I feed even the sparrows. Will I not provide you with all the vanilla you need?" Truly, those who trust God today shall not be disappointed tomorrow if they don't stop trusting. God's ways of showing us something are so precious and so unforgettable.

Jack's Turn

Since *"Those who trust the Lord shall not be disappointed"* is a truth that changed almost everything for our entire family, Peggy Joyce asked me to share a few of my own testimonies of times when God miraculously responded to our trusting, especially when the odds were not in our favor.

Freed from Pepsi at Last!

When Peggy Joyce and I came back from our honeymoon, we were excited because, as we left, my father was in the final stages of selling the Pepsi Cola Bottling plant that had been in our family since before I was born. By now my father was in his sixties, and I had no desire to run the plant. Upon our return, however, we discovered that the sale had fallen through, so I decided to make the business a success until we could find another buyer. It took thirteen years for that to happen, during which God blessed me with much success, but I still knew that bottling and selling soft drinks was not my life's ambition.

Sometime in the early seventies, the New York Pepsi Company started putting undue pressure on the smaller bottling plants across Texas. Their objective was to consolidate all of them into just three large plants located in Texas, each run by the New York Parent Company. They began to make harassing phone calls to every small bottler we knew, and they also threw in unfair demands, inflated prices . . . you name it!

I was trying very hard to learn to listen to God's voice during that time, so when I heard very clearly one night the words "Write Joan Crawford," Peggy Joyce and I spent all the next day composing a letter. Ms. Crawford's late husband, Al Steele, had been the CEO of the Pepsi Company, and she owned enough shares of Pepsi stock so that her input made a difference. We had also met and visited with her at various Pepsi Conventions.

The letter we wrote simply gave some background on a number of the older pioneer bottlers in Texas (including my father), the troubles my father had gone through in the early days to sell Pepsi against tremendous odds, the harassment we were being put through now in an attempt to get us to practically give our company away, and the failure to send us product. The letter contained a wealth of information that very few people could have known. It was a real temptation to be disappointed when we never got a response from Ms. Crawford, especially since I thought I had heard from God to write the letter.

In an attempt to keep things going I worked out a lease purchase and obtained one of the first computers in Brownwood to be used for something other than just bookkeeping. That computer was quite impressive looking—so large that it practically filled the sales office—but what made it unique was that it made sales tickets for every stop on the route, computerizing our entire sales territory, which covered fourteen counties. Computerizing sales tickets for an entire territory doesn't sound like much now, but in 1972 that was unheard of. In fact, it was that computer that caught the interest of a larger bottler, providing us with a serious potential buyer.

Meanwhile, the unfair tactics of the parent company had already put most of the small Texas bottlers out of business, and it had crippled us financially so badly that we suddenly had almost no cash flow. In turn, the cash crunch looked as though it would be our area of defeat, since one stipulation of the sale was that we have all the current bills paid in full. What would have been an easy requirement the previous year now looked like an impossibility. I knew this buyer was probably our only hope to escape liquidation, but I could see no way of coming up with the money to take care of the current bills.

Far Richer Than He Knew

After I spent two days of hard pondering and praying, the computer salesman came into my office and said, "I wish I were as rich as you." Given our situation at that moment, I had a hard time seeing the humor until I realized that he was serious. He then handed me a check for $10,000, saying that we had made a double down payment on the computer. I argued that I knew we had not, but he insisted that the check was ours and left.

In short order I found out that he was right! When we bought the computer the company had made a mistake by writing the purchase contract as lease, which did not require the $10,000 down payment we had made, instead of a lease-purchase. They had not discovered their mistake until the day before we needed the money, making the sales rep's visit supernaturally timely.

At the last moment of the 11th hour God miraculously put into our hands the $10,000 we so desperately needed. I cannot tell you the relief I felt, being able to face that buyer with every current bill marked "Paid."

In my eagerness to sell the plant I then came down off the price I was asking, and the moment the words came out of my mouth I knew I was wrong. So you can imagine how devastated I was when they turned down my lower price.

During the break I headed out to pray, fully not expecting what I heard. I was to tell them, "Since you didn't accept my offer to sell at a lower price, I am going back to the original asking price." A surprised hush just filled the room when I dropped that bomb. Then it was my turn to be surprised when they accepted the original, much higher price, with no further discussion.

After the papers were signed, my lawyer asked what I had on them that made them agree to the original price without even an argument. I was still mystified, so I gave him permission to ask them why. I almost shouted when he came back with a puzzled look on his face and said, "It was the letter you wrote to Joan Crawford. The New York lawyers were told to buy your plant at any price."

Their refusal to accept my offer, when out of fear I had lowered the asking price, was a ploy to see just how low we would go. When I shocked them by going back to a higher number, instead of further lowering the price as they expected, the thought game ended instantly and they did what they'd been told to do—to buy at any price!

God had brought about another miracle. There was no room for disappointment. I couldn't even be disappointed over the thirteen years I had spent running the plant when I realized how much God had taught me during that time—financial management, people management, sales, refrigeration, advertising, and construction. Practically everything I needed to know about building and running a church, radio stations, schools, and bookstores I had already experienced during those thirteen years. Even the training to hear God's voice had come during those years. Praise His mighty name!

The Mustard-Colored Suburban

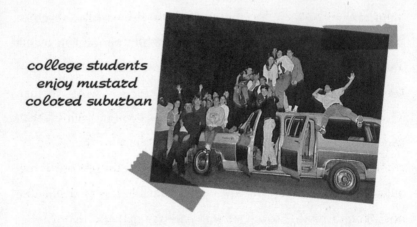

college students
enjoy mustard
colored suburban

I have even seen this truth—*Those who trust the Lord will not be disappointed*—become a reality when a situation didn't start out in trust.

Right after selling the Pepsi plant I was feeling good, and I got to reasoning that I deserved one of those new 1974 Suburbans that Chevrolet had just introduced. So without talking to Peggy Joyce or consulting with God, I walked in and bought the sales manager's one-month-old, fully equipped demo.

The first time that Peggy Joyce knew anything about it was when I wheeled into the driveway with this big Cheshire cat grin on my face. I don't think I responded very well when she asked whether I had prayed about it. But the answer to that question became obvious when I started having all kinds of problems with the car before even a week had passed.

On closer inspection I discovered a deep dent on the inside at the back of the Suburban, fresh welding underneath, and a damaged radiator, all indicating that it must have been in some kind of accident. Plus, it got less than seven miles to the gallon and had only a twenty gallon tank. In Texas that would hardly take you between towns.

My heart sank when I realized that I'd bought a lemon that had more than likely been wrecked. It was hard to trust God to come through when I knew the problem evolved from operating outside His will. But I had learned a valuable lesson that I did not want to repeat, so my repentance was genuine. Even so, I was trusting God to forgive me but righting my wrong was a little more than I could bring myself to expect.

So, I went back to the car dealership hoping to work something out, never dreaming that my check would still be in their cash drawer and would be handed back to me without an argument. When God says, "Trust Me and you will not be disappointed!" it is hard to believe the extreme measures He will take to fulfill His promises.

Then, to top that miracle, I was driving home from work about five months later when God said, "You can get your Suburban now." More than two hundred thousand miles later, the car that God okayed is still going. It has been everything the other one wasn't. On occasion, I still see it on the streets of Brownwood, being driven by a proud, antique car collector. Both my son and my son-in-law tease me about my old wood-grained, mustard-colored Suburban, but it is much more to me than just a car—it is a symbol of God's faithfulness.

Miracle from Germany

It's hard to allow your children to grow up and begin having life experiences of their own. As fathers, we would often like to keep them under our supervision all the time, but thank goodness for the grace God gives us to loosen the reins a little so they can grow up.

Bill called us from Tulsa one time, to tell us that the German class he was taking at Oral Roberts University was offering a college-accredited trip to Germany. Once the trip was officially over, before he flew back he then decided to get a week's extension so he could stay over, buy a used car, and have it shipped home.

Bill had intended to buy a BMW, but before he left on the trip God had given him a vision of a white, gasoline-driven Mercedes. He had seen an exact picture in his mind. So, even though one course in German does not necessarily make one a fluent linguist, Bill began his search in Munich, doing his best to communicate with the people and trusting in the Lord to help him survive.

Because of limited funds, Bill stayed in communal dorms with druggies and crazies and stashed complimentary breakfast rolls in his pockets for the rest of the day. And to add to the pressure, he was carrying the cash he would need to buy the car.

Only God could have overcome all the obstacles that Bill had in front of him. Within a day or two He took him to the exact, beautiful white Mercedes that Bill had seen in his vision. Bill then overcame the language barrier, correctly specified the modifications that the USDOT required, and filled out the paperwork not only to purchase the car but also to ship it home.

With his objective accomplished and his money exhausted, there was nothing to do but go to the airport and wait. Paying the financial penalty for catching an earlier flight was out of the question, so he slept there in the airport for 72 hours, stretched out like a snow angel on his luggage to keep it from being stolen. It was one totally exhausted young man who emerged from that 747 in the Dallas-Forth Worth airport, after his hair raising fifteen-day adventure. Then came the three-month wait while his car cruised across the Atlantic.

As the arrival time grew closer, Bill decided to contact the company branch office in California. No words can describe the temptation to be disappointed that came when the telephone operator told Bill there was no branch office in California by that name.

He said that disappointing thoughts of every shape, form, and fashion raced through his mind as he faced the very real possibility that the company he had dealt with in Germany might be a sham. What could he then do—fly back to Germany and say, "I want my money back?" The whole family joined in to assure the Lord, "We are trusting you, Lord, and we won't be disappointed."

It was a day of rejoicing indeed, when the call came that Bill's Mercedes was scheduled to dock at Florida in the next few weeks. The company branch office in California had taken on a different spelling of their name to give it a more Americanized sound. We wanted to say, "Forget the way it sounds—just be available!"

The occasion was so special that the entire family, including the grandmothers from both sides, took vacation time and drove to Florida to pick up the car. It was worth it all to be present to see the gleam in Bill's eyes as he walked around that car, inspecting every square inch. We had once again experienced the truth of God's Word that says, *"Those who trust the Lord shall not be disappointed."*

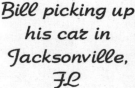

Bill picking up his car in Jacksonville, FL

I don't think it was any accident that we just happened to be coming back through New Orleans on the 25th anniversary of our wedding—the place where we had spent our honeymoon, and where God had started us on the walk of faith journey that led up to this car and every other miracle that we had experienced.

All the Land Belongs to God!

A number of years ago, while I was sitting at our front cattle tank overlooking the two hundred seventeen acres of land in the valley across the road, God simply spoke in my spirit that I could buy a tractor in December, and after that, this land. Since a neighbor had already offered the Savings and Loan Company $1000 an acre, I didn't see a way in the world for us to get the land. Yet the same excitement rose up on the inside that I had felt at previous times when God had spoken something to me.

I told Peggy Joyce what I had heard, but there was little I could do except put it on a shelf and wait. When I was able to miraculously get my John Deere tractor in December (which is a whole story all by itself), just as God had promised, my faith was greatly encouraged.

It was probably a couple of months later when we heard that the Savings and Loan Company that was handling the land had refused the $1000-an-acre offer, and then later had declared bankruptcy. The Resolution Trust Corporation (RTC) took over the sale of the land, and I felt God leading me to submit a bid. I reasoned that I had to bid more than $1000 since that amount had already been refused.

I'll digress a moment before I finish my story. When I was working for the FMC Company they offered to match whatever an employee put into FMC stock. Miraculously, I had received a $1000 annual pay raise, and I felt like God impressed me to invest the raise in FMC stock. I did that for the seven years that I was with the company. In those seven years the stock split five to one and went from $12 to $66 a share.

With the money from the sale of that stock, and what I was able to borrow from my brother-in-law's GI loan, I submitted a bid that was one-third of what the Savings and Loan Company that went bankrupt had refused the year before, but it was the best I could come up with. Needless to say, the bid was turned down flat. Interestingly, when I prayed I felt like the Lord said, "You bid too much. Bid again with what money you actually have without borrowing."

As crazy as it seemed, I was obedient and submitted a much lower bid to the realtor who was negotiating for us. He thought we had lost our minds and didn't hesitate to tell us. In fact, I don't think he ever even submitted the bid, so Bill called the RTC directly and found that the man who had previously handled our account had been replaced.

After a long conversation the new officer verbally accepted our $240-an-acre bid right there on the phone. Bill and I were both beside ourselves with joy. Owning that land was like a dream come true. We knew that only by the grace of God had that happened. God had given me the pay raise to invest in the first place, so if I bought the land for $240 an acre, that land would be entirely a gift from God— actually costing me nothing.

At that point, everything had come together like clockwork so we were puzzled when the c losing kept being postponed, time after time. It was almost too late to rectify the situation when we found out that the realtor was furious that the guy at RTC had settled for such a ridiculously low price. Knowing that our agreement was verbal, he was delaying the closing until he could get another buyer in place who was willing to pay a great deal more.

By the time we realized what had happened it looked like a done deal in his favor. The RTC may have discredited our offer, thinking we were the ones who were delaying the closing. Whatever the reason, it appeared that the land had slipped through our fingers. Disappointment was definitely knocking at our door. I don't know what might have happened had we taken the time to wallow in that for a day or two. But instead, Bill jumped in the car, bypassed the realtor altogether, made a flying trip to the RTC office in Dallas, explained the underhanded scheme that was going on, and insisted that the man honor the verbal agreement that he had made. Within just a few hours the deal was closed. Needless to say, the realtor was not a very happy camper, but once again God had intervened in a marvelous way and we were not disappointed.

Merrit and Cullen on the land God gave us.

KPSM, the Rock, and KBUB Christian Radio

Transmitter building and Radio tower
The `ready to be installed` beacon in the
foreground is the 90% cost saving warning light
that God provided for the top the
500 foot radio tower.

After many years of Peggy Joyce's teaching locally in our church and at different seminars, I thought many more people could benefit from the truths she had been sharing if we put her weekly Bible study on the air. So, for the greater part of a year, Angelia and I called radio stations in Brownwood and Abilene to find out what it would cost. That had been a long time goal as another means of getting the Word of God to people outside the four walls of the church. The cost seemed prohibitive but the idea was not forgotten; just placed on a back burner for the time being.

Not long afterward, Peggy Joyce was teaching in San Antonio at the home of Ron and Lynne Williams, when a handsome, well-dressed man came in and sat in the back row. An altar call for salvation was not the norm in these meetings because she was usually addressing an all-Christian group, but in this particular meeting she broke protocol by asking if there was anyone who would like to receive the Lord as his Savior. To my surprise, this man raised his hand and left the meeting that day a new creation in Christ.

A few months later the same man sent an envelope to her ministry, containing a large check designated for radio. You can imagine our excitement, but to my surprise every door seemed to c lose. We finally put the money into a savings account until we could clearly get the Lord's direction.

When a radio station came up for sale in Brownwood we felt the Lord saying, "Buy it!" We were plunged immediately into a state of shock—and that's putting it mildly! How were we supposed to know how to run a radio station? If we had ever been tempted to ignore God's voice it was then. Peggy Joyce said that half of her was too excited to breathe and the other half was too scared. I think it was a wonder she didn't pass out from lack of oxygen during those next few weeks.

We were looking for confirmation, so when we hired a youth pastor at the church whose whole background had been in radio, you can imagine how the excitement mounted. Another confirmation came when we found that the price of the station was the exact amount of the check that had been given to us earlier.

Radio talk dominated our conversations for the next few weeks until we finally took the big leap and signed the papers. It was hard not to have our spirits dampened a little as we waded through all of the requirements from the FCC, to get the license transferred from the previous owner who had gone bankrupt. But finally the big day came when we were ready to go on the air.

Is the War Over Yet?

Sometimes we forget that we are still in a war zone and need to keep our battle clothes on and our armor secure. It's not quite time to put on the wedding gown, as there seems to always be a new giant to conquer. Just as we were ready to go on the air, a local, non-commercial, Christian radio station on our tower, which was owned and operated out of Dallas, filed a petition against our commercial station.

Long before the petition was filed, we had called them to say that we wanted to work with them, and we even offered them free tower space and electricity— but they obviously did not want to work with us. Word got back to us that they had said, "We intend to get them off the air and cost them a lot of money before it's over."

Half of their goal was achieved! For the next year we paid out more money in FCC lawyer fees than I want to remember, plus having to endure the emotional stress of dealing with the situation. Many times we questioned whether we had heard correctly to buy the station. At times it was really hard to muster up the strength to say, "Lord, we are trusting You, and we won't be disappointed," but we knew that God was our only hope. Almost exactly one year and many thousands of dollars later, the petition was lifted and our station went officially on the air.

Sometimes we wonder how God can ever bring good out of certain things, but His ways are so much higher than our ways. Three years later this sister station dismissed the Dallas employees who had caused us so much grief and happily blessed us, free-of charge, with the very non-commercial station that they had tried so hard to protect. This enabled us to have a contemporary Christian music station for the younger audience, and a praise and teaching Christian station for other ages. Praise be to His Name!

God's miracles on those two radio stations have never ceased. With every opportunity to be disappointed, God has never failed to honor our trust. When the main computer that runs the radio went down, we sent it in to be refurbished. The replacement computer, costing $25,000 with all its software, was shipped to us, but, through an oversight by the company, it was insured for only $2,500.

Obviously, the enemy must have spotted his opportunity, because a warehouse worker drove the blade of a forklift right through the computer and utterly destroyed it. Suddenly, we found ourselves with a major opportunity to be disappointed. We had barely come up with the money for the update— much less enough to buy a new computer, which was now selling for $31,000.

Every avenue we tried led to a dead end. For days we kept confessing out loud, "Lord, we are trusting You—we refuse to go by sight." Sight can seem so overwhelming at times. We kept confessing our trust that God would make a way for us to stay on the air. We knew we could not afford to let down for a moment, because it is so easy to waver when we encounter a situation that seems to have no alternatives.

I tried to think of a solution but there seemed to be none. The bank wouldn't even consider that kind of loan. However, I had made an appointment to see our CPA about another matter, and when the radio problem came up in conversation he suggested that we check with our own insurance company.

Not only were we covered, but they had a check in our hands before the day was up. Had the bank loaned us the money we would still be making payments. God will work a way when there is no way, if we will trust Him

Come into My Coffee House

From house to coffee house

Another of our blessings that tested our trust on numerous occasions, before the not being-disappointed part came, was the college coffee house.

The sixty-plus University students who packed into our son-in-law and daughter's home every Tuesday night for Bible study were bursting the seams. The answer was not in finding another place to meet, since their on-campus house was so easily accessible. But after exploring various possibilities—none of which worked—we were back at ground zero.

Time passed, and a little ninety-six-year-old lady, who owned the only other on-campus house, went home to be with the Lord. Buying that home and remodeling it into a coffee house would serve as a multi-purpose answer to our dilemma. But nothing could have prepared us for all the obstacles that lay ahead. It was a trust walk all the way.

The price was extremely high and we didn't have the money to buy it, let alone to remodel it! Thinking that borrowing the money was my only solution, I called the bank's attention to the fact that the asking price was well over the tax-appraised value, but they assured me that would not be a problem since we were going to remodel and add restrooms and a kitchen on the back. However, when it came time to sign the paperwork, the bank reneged and wouldn't loan more than the amount of the appraisal.

Beth, a precious niece of the lady who died, was the executrix of the will and she was more than willing to work with us, but she also had the other relatives to consider. Our bright idea to see if they would owner-finance the amount over what we could borrow at the bank was received with an emphatic "No!"

However, on one occasion when we were talking to Beth, Angelia and I were scheduled to cook hamburgers and minister to the boys at the Texas Youth Prison in Brownwood. Since Beth was from out of town and we were running late, we just invited her to go with us, which she very graciously agreed to do.

Meanwhile, nothing went right. We were cooking the hamburgers outside in 105-degree weather with no place for Beth to get any shade, and the wind blew smoke over her and the boys, thus preventing us from ministering to them. The evening looked like a disaster. It was hard not to be disappointed, considering that this fiasco had probably driven Beth even farther away from any kind of business agreement.

But just as we felt ourselves running out of options, Beth and her husband gave us a word that was nothing short of a miracle. They were still unwilling to owner-finance, but they would be willing to drop the price of the house down to what we could pay. We could not believe our ears. That was the miracle we needed. Clearly, God knows when we get battle weary and discouraged, but He also knows that one of His miracles can give us enough joy to put any hint of disappointment on the run!

At the signing of the papers, Beth told us something else that surprised and thrilled us. She said, "The reason I sold you the house was because I could see that your ministry was real when I went with you to the youth prison." On that particular night it had seemed to us to be more futile than real, but God does work in mysterious ways.

Power That's Always Current

Our first big hurdle had been passed, but what faced us was going to take just as much of a miracle. Because of the city codes, ADA restrooms, off the street parking, as well as a great many other things— the remodeling costs and the time it took to do the work spiraled to double what I had anticipated. Since we were still in the middle of constructing the multi-purpose building on our church property, we were needing every spare nickel for that project. So, as I watched the college house absorbing money as if it were a sponge, depression really tried to set in.

Depression has become a check system for me. I have come to realize that when I'm depressed I am not trusting. That is my clue to repent and start trusting all over again. On the other hand, when we think things are about as bad as they can get, they sometimes get worse before they get better!

Some of the men from our church were helping with the construction when suddenly we all heard a loud explosion. Fire began flying out the top of the power pole, and steam came pouring out of the hole in which two of the men were standing, ankle-deep in water from the previous night's rain. One of the men had been holding onto a metal stake while the other man drove it into the ground, and they accidentally drove it into the main electric power line, knocking all the electricity out for blocks around and shooting fire in all directions.

The Texas Utilities Electric people were stunned. Seven thousand, two hundred volts of electricity were flowing through the line into which our guys had just driven the metal stake. According to the electricians there should have been nothing left of our men except two little pieces of charcoal. None of the officials could believe that anyone could have survived what happened, especially while holding onto the metal and standing in water.

They reminded us that only a few months before, two men who were cutting tree limbs away from the power lines, with far less contact than what these two men experienced, had been electrocuted, and their truck and equipment burned completely to a crisp. The years of quoting Psalm 91 over our church body had certainly paid off.

It was obvious that the enemy had tried to hit two targets at once—the college house, as well as a ministry project that was scheduled to take place that very afternoon in front of the college house. The World's Strongest Man, Tony Clark with Champions for Life, was coming in that afternoon to lift a Ford Escort car like a wheelbarrow and walk it ten feet. Our radio station, The Rock, was doing a remote of the event, and several hundred people came—many of whom were saved that afternoon. No wonder satan was fighting us so hard, trying to get us to be disappointed and quit.

No one could deny the miracles that were happening, but that didn't change the fact that I was still a great deal over budget. But God has a plan even when we can't see a way. Months later, two families from out of town sent checks— without even knowing we had such an enormous need— paying for the entire remodeling job at the coffee house.

Sometimes it is impossible to know the battles that people are going through by just looking on the surface, but by trusting God we can be guaranteed a victory. When I see that college house, now completed and all decorated university style, with hundreds of students ministering and being ministered to, I can hardly contain my emotions. It then becomes easy to trust in a God who cares about us more than we care about ourselves.

The things I have written are just the tip of the iceberg. I would love to share with you miracles I experience on an almost daily basis, of times when God has taken what Satan meant for evil and turned it to a miracle for good—when I trusted Him.

But simply telling stories isn't the point—my most fervent desire is to let you know that this revelation will work for you, when you discover how easy it is to trust an amazing Father who handles even the most minuté details. The next time you face a challenge, I dare you to get excited about trusting God to make a way when there is no way.

before remodeling for coffee house

coffee house after remodeling

I suspect you might be surprised, even now, to recall how many times God has already worked miracles on your behalf when you trusted Him.

Epilogue

As we became stronger in the truths of God's Word, my husband was called into full-time ministry. In 1979, he helped to found, build, and pastor our interdenominational church, Living Word Church, located on eighteen acres of beautiful land covered with pecan trees and situated on the banks of the Pecan Bayou, just outside Brownwood, Texas. Our church has a Christian Academy with students pre-K through high school, a daycare program, a full power FM K-99 Christian radio station called THE ROCK, a KBUB listener-supported praise and teaching radio station, a bookstore, a nursing home ministry, a prison ministry, a deliverance ministry, and other in-reach and outreach ministries. Jack and several men in the church built the 21,500 square-foot auditorium before he retired from full-time pastoring to travel with our new ministry endeavors.

*This is the new auditorium,
21,500 sq ft. It is finished now
and cost just over $500,000, and
it is really first class. God did
another miracle!*

For thirty years as a pastor's wife, I taught the Wednesday night Bible studies and spoke at other church conferences. Now, as a family we travel to speak at conferences both nationally and internationally. God has also opened up many other doors of opportunity, with a recent emphasis on military speaking engagements through the Psalm 91 books, and our extended family is now involved at various levels of this ministry as well.

Our children attended Howard Payne University in Brownwood and Oral Roberts University in Tulsa. And, after returning to Brownwood, they and their spouses are very committed to the ministry. Bill is a lawyer and took care of all the legal business for the church; his wife, Sloan, is a decorator and an intercessor. Angelia and her husband, David, are the college pastors, teaching Bible truths and leading mission teams that have gone to India, Ireland, Estonia, South Africa, the Philippines, New York, San Francisco, Houston, and Israel. Angelia also manages our two Christian radio stations.

University Mission Team in Ireland

I'm so glad that as a family we learned trusting principles early on. We've come to realize that God often calls a person to do things beyond his finances. Then, as he steps out, God gives the provision. God has never failed to honor His Word. He continues to show forth the same deliverance, healing, and provision that He so powerfully demonstrated in my life and in the lives of those in my family. Time and space do not allow me to share all the miracles that we have experienced, but I'm not sure I would if I could. It's time to turn the focus back onto you, for whom His infinite love and His limitless provisions can be even more miraculous.

Trust in the Lord and you will not be disappointed!

*Heath, Jolena
and their children
Hunter Kent, Avery and Peyton*

One of the greatest gifts parents can have is for their children to follow in the ministry. Not only has God drawn our extended family to Himself according to Proverbs 22: 6, Isaiah 54:13 and Acts 16:31, but David & Angie adopted Jolena and have seen those same promises work in her life, as well. She and her husband, Heath, and their three children, Avery, Peyton and Hunter Kent, live in Montana where Heath serves in the United States Air Force. Jack and I stand amazed hearing testimonies of how Heath and Jolena minister to military families.

*For more stories about Heath, Jolena and their children, read Peggy Joyce's Psalm 91: God's Shield of Protection, Military Edition and Psalm 91 For Youth.

What Must I Do to Be Saved?

We've been talking about blessings that are available to a child of God when he trusts his Lord. These blessings can also be available to you. If you have never given your life to Jesus and accepted Him as your Lord and Savior, the invitation is open to everyone and there is no better time than right now to ask Jesus into your heart.

> *There is none righteous, not even one.*
> *(Romans 3:10)*

> *...for all have sinned and fallen short*
> *of the glory of God.   (Romans 3:23)*

God loves you and gave His life that you might live eternally with Him.

> *But God demonstrates His own love*
> *toward us, in that while we were*
> *yet sinners, Christ died for us.*
> *(Romans 5:8)*

For God so loved the world (you),
that He gave His only begotten Son,
that whoever believes in Him should not
perish but have eternal life.   (John 3:16)

There is nothing we can do to earn our salvation or to make ourselves good enough to go to heaven. It is a free gift! There is also no other avenue through which we can reach heaven, other than Jesus Christ, God's Son.

And there is salvation in no one else;
for there is no other name under heaven
that has been given among men, by
which we must be saved.   (Acts 4:12)

Jesus said to him, "I am the way,
and the Truth, and the Life; no one
comes to the Father, but through Me."
(John 14:6)

You must believe that Jesus is the Son of God, that He died on the cross for your sins, and that He rose again on the third day.

...who (Jesus) was declared with
power to be the Son of God by the
resurrection from the dead.
(Romans 1:4)

You may be thinking, "How do I accept Jesus and become His child?" God in His Love has made it so easy.

If you confess with your mouth the
Lord Jesus and believe in your heart
that God raised Him from the dead,
you shall be saved.   (Romans 10:9)

But as many as received Him,
to them He gave the right to become
children of God, even to those who
believe in His Name.   (John 1:12)

It is as simple as praying a prayer similar to this one, if you sincerely mean it in your heart:

Dear God:

I believe You gave your Son, Jesus, to die for me. I believe He shed His Blood to pay for my sins and that You raised Him from the dead so I can be Your child and live with You eternally in heaven. I am asking Jesus to come into my heart right now and save me. I confess Him as the Lord and Master of my life.

I thank You, dear Lord, for loving me enough to lay down your life for me. Take my life now and use it for Your Glory. I ask for all that You have for me.

In Jesus' Name,

Amen

About the Author

At the age of twenty-two, Peggy Joyce Ruth encountered an emotional illness that lasted for eight years. Under a psychiatrist's care for severe depression, she underwent several months of electrical shock treatments and was told that she would have to spend the rest of her life on medication just to function. But when her doctors explained to her husband that she might still wind up in an institution, he took the Bible's promises of deliverance literally and asked the Lord to intervene. At that point the Lord not only healed her completely but also set her free, in miraculous fashion, from the medications, the psychiatric care, and the fears.

Nowadays, Peggy Joyce teaches a weekly Bible study on the BETTER LIVING ministry KPSM Radio Broadcast, has a CD mail out ministry, and conducts various church and Christian group seminars. Two of her favorite experiences include teaching on a Caribbean Christian cruise ship and being elected as team cook for thirty-two HPU students on a mission trip into the Tenderloin area of San Francisco. Most recently, she has spoken at deployment conferences for the US military, has participated in Psalm 91 book distributions to overseas military bases, and has worked with chaplains to fulfill requests to distribute her books into strategic military zones in Iraq, Afghanistan, Kuwait, Korea, Kosovo, Israel, the Philippines, and other parts of the world.

Since her deliverance from the bondage of emotional illness, for more than thirty years Peggy Joyce Ruth has shared her experiences and served as living proof that God can do the impossible—and that His Word is relevant for today to meet every need. Peggy Joyce believes that, and after reading this book, you will have more personal testimonies in your life of how God is worthy of your trust.

If you have a trust testimony you would like to share, please contacts us at: www.peggyjoyceruth.org

For speaking engagements, Peggy Joyce can be contacted at 325-646-3420, 325-646-6894 or at 325-646 0623.

HEAR PEGGY JOYCE !!!!

To LISTEN to this **audio message** by
Peggy Joyce Ruth,
Those Who Trust in the Lord
Shall Not Be Disappointed
as well as other teachings including
Psalm 91
Peggy Joyce's Testimony,
please visit
www.peggyjoyceruth.org

All of her teachings may be downloaded
for your own personal use.

Psalm 91:
God's Shield of Protection

New Expanded Version of the
Military Edition with more
testimonies Including Psalm 91
Stories from Firemen, Policemen
and Prison Guards Published by
Charisma Publishing Co This book is
ideal for anyone whose job is putting him
in harm's way. The testimonies in this
book will thrill your heart while they
demonstrate the love of the Lord &

the awesomeness of His power like never before. **The
examples in this book are for those in military or live
around constant danger.**

Psalm 91 Workbook
Make it Meaningful, Make it
Real, Make it Mine!

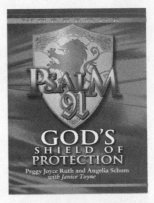

This workbook is based on the
work of Peggy Joyce Ruth's
examination of Psalm 91 through
her books Psalm 91: God's Umbrella
of Protection & Psalm 91: God's
Shield of Protection (Military). It is
divided into fifteen lessons. Each
lesson includes applicable parables or analogies to help you
think through various life events, questions to initiate
personal response to these concepts, fill-in-the-blank
questions, and projects to work as a group or as an individual.

$8.00 + S&H – **Psalm 91 book or Psalm Workbook;**
$17.99 + S&H – **Hardback Psalm 91**: Add $2 for a CD.

Order Today: www.peggyjoyceruth.org
Phone: Toll Free: (877) 97-BOOKS (877 972-6657)

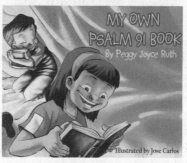

Tormented: Eight Years and Back

Tormented: Eight Years and Back is the heartwarming story of a young woman's struggle through eight tormenting years of emotional illness, electrical shock treatments, prescription drugs, and hopelessness—culminating in absolute victory made possible only by God's supernatural delivering power. It is one of the most  comprehensive books on protection from demonic forces that you will most likely ever read. Peggy Joyce Ruth tells you her personal testimony of God's delivering power and gives you scriptures to help you stay free!

Special: Add $2–*Tormented: Eight Years & Back* teaching CD $10 plus $2 shipping& handling.

Phone: 1- 877-97-BOOKS
1-877-972-6657

God's Smuggler, Jr.

by Angelia Ruth Schum
Peggy Joyce Ruth's daughter
This is the true story of someone who prayed for anything but an average life… "God, never let my life be boring!" You'll be amazed at 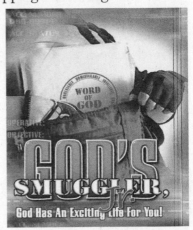 how God answered that prayer. As the story develops in an exotic place, there is nonstop action with twists and turns as Bibles are smuggled past armed guards into Communist land. This book will challenge you to pray that same prayer without stipulations: "God, please don't ever let my life be boring!"

$8 + $2 shipping & handling. Call 1-877-972-6657.

TO ORDER ADDITIONAL COPIES

of

Those Who Trust in the Lord

Shall Not Be Disappointed!

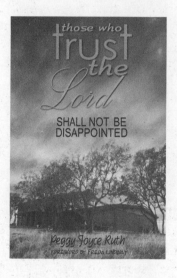

CALL TODAY

and get a copy for a friend!

Call 325-646-6894 or 1-877-97-books (1-877-972-6657)
$8 + $2 shipping & handling.
or ORDER through www.peggyjoyceruth.org